The Spiritual UN Gentle Path

A Manifesto for Earth People to Build Love on Light

Copyrighted Material

The Spiritual UN Gentle Path: A Manifesto for Earth People to Build Love on Light

Copyright © 2011, 2012, 2013 by The Spiritual UN

All Rights Reserved.

No part of this publication may be reproduced, stored in a retrieval system or transmitted, in any form or by any means—electronic, mechanical, photocopying, recording or otherwise—without prior written permission, except for the inclusion of brief quotations in a review.

For information about this title, contact the publisher:
The Spiritual UN
P.O. Box 6537, McLean, VA 22106 USA
http://www.thespiritualun.org

978-0-615-41866-7

Printed in the United States of America

Cover and Interior design: 1106 Design

*Make gentle the life of this world.
Let us dedicate ourselves to that.*
— Robert F. Kennedy

Contents

	Introduction	vii
1	War and Terror Is Error in Natural Reality—Begin Again	1
2	No Human Being Is an Enemy of Another Human Being—The Essence of Our Humanity Is to Help Not Harm—It is the Truth and the Way	7
3	Joining Both Sides of the Divide: East Meets West and the Abolition of All War—The Five Fundamental Principles of the American Founding (West-1776 AD) Are Fundamental to Islam (East-610 AD)	15
4	The Fifth Fundamental Pivotal Principle of Both America and Islam: Money Must Be Usury-Free	25
5	How We Are to Flow Life, Liberty, Happiness and Right Progress of All of Humanity—Without Sin for Religious People, and Without Error for Rational People	39

6	Putting Money to Work for the Good Stewardship and Caring for the Planet and All People	49
7	Life, Liberty and Happiness—Money as Creative Oil	67
8	Love's Turn on the Planet—Thomas Jefferson's "Governing Ourselves without a Master" and the Advancement of All	73
9	Addendum to Love's Turn on the Planet— An Economic System That Serves Humanity	83
10	The God-Forward of Evolution and the Pro-Human Way of Life Through the Holistic World Planetary Paradigm of The Spiritual UN — Wholeness, Oneness and our Union Magnified	103
	The Spiritual UN Conceptual Index	131
	The Spiritual UN Gentle Path Thesis	181

Introduction

THE HOLISTIC WORLD planetary paradigm centers our world on the importance of the whole of Life and the interdependence of its parts. It allows us the choice to turn toward a Warless and a totally toxic-free world by laying down, in *terra firma,* a new plan and pattern on the Planet where no Human being is an enemy of another Human being.

This book is the culmination of a highly inspired, spiritually-based thought structure that strips away our artificial divides and labels to reveal our Humanity and return us to our essential function as Human beings—which is simply to help each other and all Life on the Planet in a dynamic and progressive way. It draws beautifully from our Higher or better nature—the center of our Heart nature—orienting us toward a totally new life and pattern on the Planet which *feels like Home.*

We are placed directly in the spiritual truth of the Unity and Oneness of all Life with harm or violence to none, upholding life, evolution and enlightenment in our Life on Earth and in all the ways we live and exist together on the Earth.

It puts to rest the argument that Islam is the West's enemy, or anyone's enemy, when in fact it is the blueprint of the American Founding itself. At the same time, as the fundamental basis of both Islam and America, it liberates money to perform its proper function of simply meeting all of Humanity's Human needs (in contrast to the world of Wars and institutionalized violence) so that we are *all—everywhere*—equally able to have the opportunity to reach our full evolutionary potential and creativity. As a direct result, we have eliminated world poverty, hunger and collective slave-like toil in system-induced meaningless lives for millions (all of us Humans) everywhere.

It draws on the truth of Occam's Razor that states that simplicity is our best way forward, or that we should not create unnecessary complications through our governing structure—we need only a set of principles defined with absolute clarity that govern us in a perfect and perfecting way that opens us all to growth and evolution within ourselves and within our world.

Most of all, the book allows us to move from authoritarianism to a place, in the words of Thomas Jefferson, of "governing ourselves without master" with our weight rightly shifted onto (and into) our spiritual, transcendental or divine element which the teachings of all Religions and wisdom traditions have given to us *for us* throughout time for the complete and essential existence of all Life on Earth—and for knowing who we are.

Introduction

With all in the open and in our spiritual consciousness as the liberating force, we have completed the American Experiment that Life, Liberty and Happiness—a condition universally desired by all Human beings—is possible for all on Earth in our magnificent individuality.

In truth and respect of all,
Sherrii

1 War and Terror Is Error in Natural Reality—Begin Again

Mankind must put an end to war,
or war will put an end to mankind.
— John F. Kennedy

IT IS SAID THAT TRUE SPIRITUALITY seeks to re-unite a thread that connects all of us to the rest of life—and thus brings us together—and it is in this truth that we find the basis of the American Declaration of Independence as the only true and acceptable reality to the Human Race:

> "We hold these truths to be self-evident, that all men are created equal, that they are endowed by their Creator with certain unalienable Rights, that among these are Life, Liberty, and the pursuit of Happiness."

The lead paragraph of the Declaration of Independence mandates that the above reality is our Natural Reality, and that anything that corrupts the existence of it must essentially be made null and void:

> *"When in the Course of human events, it becomes necessary for one people to dissolve the political bands which have connected them with another, and to assume among the powers of the earth, the separate and equal station to which the Laws of Nature and of Nature's God entitle them, a decent respect to the opinions of mankind requires that they should declare the causes which impel them to the separation."*

The current world reality of War and Terror speaks for itself, which is nothing but violence, error, and a corruption of our Natural Reality. This means that we Humans have deviated from the path of Natural Reality and are living in an illusion and a lie or an *Error Reality.*

At the same time, Natural Reality, i.e., "We hold these truths to be self-evident . . ." of the American Declaration of Independence, is a whole and complete world in and of itself—spiritually rooted, grounded, and founded on spiritual principles and ideals. Expanding and translating those spiritual principles and ideals are the other two Founding Documents, the Bill of Rights and the Constitution which are its supports.

However, when the supports themselves have "disappeared" to give the effect of Error Reality through War and Terror, we must turn back to the Source of Natural Reality. The Source of Natural Reality is God who is aligned and corresponds to the manifestations of Natural Reality: Fullness of Equality, Life, Liberty, Truth, Rights and Happiness *for all*—which deems it a Universal Reality that has risen above the artificial concept and construct of "nationality" (because we are ultimately and essentially all Human beings).

Because the American Declaration of Independence and its supports are a stand-alone Reality connected to Source (Creator) they can be channeled through a spiritually rooted, grounded and founded Universal Reality to **begin again.**

As The Spiritual UN itself connects with the foundational essence of all the wisdom and teachings of the great Philosophies and Religions that are Universal in nature and are connected to Source (Creator),[1] it can take on the task of the perfect unfoldment of Natural Reality (i.e. "We hold these truths to be self-evident . . . .") of the American Declaration of Independence with the end result being the perfect conclusion of the American Experiment itself:

> *I have no fear that the result of our experiment will be that men may be trusted to govern themselves without a master.*
> — Thomas Jefferson

At the same time, The Spiritual UN chooses the wholeness of the spiritual path as it re-aligns the American

---

[1] The Holistic World Planetary Paradigm of The Spiritual UN reconnects us with the underlying unity and oneness of all Life: http://www.thespiritualun.org

Experiment to fulfill the Hopi Prophecy of God's Promise to Humanity as it had been foretold:

> *"The great Spirit or Creator meets man. The Creator then gave man the Sacred Circle, a promised life of peace and plenty if, and only if, man would follow the spiritual path.*
>
> *"The Hopi were to look to the East for the return of their lost white brother, for he was to bring a missing stone tablet to complement the one they already had.*
>
> *"As the brown man waited, the white man travelled the Earth on a mission to spread the spiritual circle and return with knowledge. Instead of the circle he brought the symbol of the cross."*[2]

Looking East from the North American continent stands Europe which is how the Hopi Prophecy was referring to the culture of the White Man. The symbol of the cross is therefore, not directly referring to the religion of Christianity, but a disconnect from the Oneness of all life through the culture of materialism and modernism. The White Man has concentrated his knowledge on technological advances without taking into consideration and assimilation the sanctity and integrity of all life as

---

[2] Thomas Banyacya, Hopi elder delivering message to world: http://www.thespiritualun.org/Hopi_Prophecy.htm

the Native Americans knew it (and all other indigenous peoples of the Earth knew it).

Being devoid of full knowledge, the White Man proceeds with technological advances and, from the thirst for power, creates Wars which create two possible pathways or destinies on the Planet that Man can choose:

Possibility One: The Violent and Violate Life, which is:

1) An inevitable self-destruction through a breached life on the Planet that leads to more war, disease, death and catastrophic destruction through technological arrogance, ignorance and consequent imbalance with the Earth, or

Possibility Two: The True or Gentle Life, which is:

2) Peace and plenty for all as the Promised Life of the Creator through the knowledge of the Sacred Circle as the Oneness and Wholeness of all Life on the spiritual path.

As The Spiritual UN chooses the spiritual path, it makes the conscious choice to join the two tablets of the Hopi Prophecy—the ancient knowledge with the modern world—so that we may continue to exist on the Planet without the end to all life and civilization through catastrophic destruction, and at the same time, complete the American Experiment with Peace and Plenty for All as our Natural Reality and Existence.

How we get there is no longer through the old conceptual paradigm or world construct, with its constant anticipation of "Fear"-events and realities, but through Love—a truer, bolder and better Reality that is closer to home—presenting itself through the world of Beauty, Truth, Justice and Wisdom as an *indivisible Whole* where each is the other. The palpable effect will be the Happiness of all through the forward momentum of Humanity in a planet-wide evolutionary consciousness that is good to all and advances all.

In the two possible pathways of the Hopi Prophecy of "Peace and Plenty for all" or "Catastrophic and Total Destruction," we, as Humanity, must consciously choose and help build the spiritual path as an end to War and disharmony with the Earth and all her people because it is an Error in the mode of our Natural Reality.

2 No Human Being Is an Enemy of Another Human Being—The Essence of Our Humanity Is to Help Not Harm—It is the Truth and the Way

Function according to your form.
— Aristotle

REMEMBER THE JOURNALIST Kevin Carter whose photo of a vulture looking toward and not far from a small child during the 1994 Sudan famine won him the Pulitzer Prize? The vulture was stalking the famine-stricken toddler as he or she was crawling in the direction of a United Nations food camp which was a kilometer away. Kevin left as soon as the photo was taken but later confided to friends that he wished he had intervened. However, journalists at the time were warned not to touch the victims of famine for fear of disease. Three months later, and only weeks after being awarded the Pulitzer Prize, Kevin committed suicide.

What happened to Kevin? Why would he want to commit suicide right after receiving such a prestigious award? It seems there is an anomaly, and to find what it could be we have to reach further into our souls to know—and that was literally done by some Rishis, or some very wise men many thousands of years ago in ancient India, whose only purpose was to find Human purpose in the world, which they did by turning inwardly through meditation. These sages gave to the world an enlightened body of knowledge that developed and evolved over several hundred years of what was known as the Vedic period of ancient India. What had been discovered by them was that the fundamental essence of a Human being is to help and not to harm—and is illustrated by the following story:

> *"A sage, seated beside the Ganges, notices a scorpion that has fallen into the water. He reaches down and rescues it, only to be stung. Some time later he sees the scorpion thrashing about in the water again. Once more he reaches down to rescue it, and once more he is stung. A bystander, observing all this, exclaims, 'Holy one, why do you keep doing that? Don't you see that the wretched creature will only sting you in return?' 'Of course,' the sage replied. 'It is the dharma of a scorpion to sting. But it is the dharma of a human being to save.'"*[3]

"Dharma" comes from the Sanskrit root word *dhri*, which means to support, hold up, or bear. In its essential

---

[3] *The Bhagavad Gita*, Eknath Easwaran (1985, 2007 by the Blue Mountain Center of Meditation), 31–32

meaning it implies "support from within," the essence of a thing, its virtue, that is, its moral excellence or what makes it the best that it is. If we merged the meanings within the context of life or Creation, the closest we will come to in its actual meaning is *essential function*. Thus, just as it is the dharma of a Human being to help or, more pointedly, to save, the dharma of a scorpion is to sting, which at the same time rightly shifts or removes all creatures of the natural world from the real meaning of evil—*"every creature of God is good"* (1 Timothy 4:4).

As Human beings, "dharma" means our soul purpose which fits the self and the world perfectly as one growing Whole, literally. When we are in our dharma or soul purpose we are expanding ourselves and the world at the same time as though we are One. The experience to be experienced as feedback is bliss, joy and fulfillment, not only with ourselves but the whole experience itself serves as a contribution to the world in the most delightful and wholesome way that advances all—*without harm, i.e. harmless.*

On the other hand, when we are not in our soul purpose or dharma, we experience the contrasting reality of karma—which we know contains the negative effects of suffering, pain, dissolution and despair. The world itself, it seems, is nothing but a karmic reality giving those effects for all life on the Planet. We are all suffering, Human, animal, plant and mineral life through pain, dislocation and harm because we Human beings are not in our dharma or soul essence of helping all and harming none.

Our dharma or soul purpose gives us the right fit for the world, or to make us, literally, fit for life. It is the same meaning as when Socrates said, "An unreflective life is not worth living." Without living through our reflective or creative selves we are karmically implicated in a backward cycle and inertness—or a self destructive state that can best be described by a law of physics, the Second Law of Thermodynamics, which is an expression of the (materialist) universal principle of decay observable in Nature. A property and measurement of this expression is "entropy," which is the degree to which a system is in disequilibrium or disorder—eventually leading to its dissolution and total destruction.

On our physical or material level, an unreflective life is the karmic life—a life out of our dharma or soul purpose with its attendant entropy. War and terror is in the same system of entropy because it contains all the karmic or observable effects: the experience of pain, suffering, dissolution and despair—which tell us that the world itself is not fitting itself to or founding itself on what it means to be Human, i.e. "to save" or "to help."

In the system of War, through a law of physics, we are dooming ourselves to *certain* destruction, regardless, for example, of what is taking place on the surface reality through words and manipulation for pre-determined or pre-set agendas. John F. Kennedy aptly caught the whole system of War in a nutshell:

> *"Mankind must put an end to war, or war will put an end to Mankind."*

Nothing could be truer. Our natural existence as Human beings is to save or help all, and harm none. Through our dharma or soul purpose we are born to help not harm the world, and that is how we are to exist, which manifests itself in a sacred manner or way. War is thus an unnatural existence of the Human Race—it is the wrong fit or foundation for our soul and consequently the world. In theological terms the "wrong fit" for the Human soul is understood as "sin"—which means error. Through War or "perpetual war" we are living an *error existence.*

On another more personal level, we see Kevin—because of an environment of fear, i.e., he was warned not to touch the victims of famine for fear of disease—lost or ignored his essential function or soul purpose as a Human being of helping (not harming), which can and does happen to us all. When we go against our essential function, our soul purpose—the very grain of our being that makes us Human or essentially what we are—we find we cannot live with ourselves in equilibrium. Is it any wonder why there are a very high number of suicides and mental breakdowns in the military?[4] It is because we Human beings are not meant for war and killing one

---

[4] Going against the unity of all life means that you will, literally, lose your own: "Suicide Claims More U.S. Military Lives Than Afghan War," James Cogan: http://www.wsws.org/articles/2010/jan2010/suic-j06.shtml and also, *"The war robbed us of human dignity and stole away our humanity so we reached for drugs to help us deny all that"* from "Still Falls the Rain," John J. McCullagh:
http://www.catholicireland.net/pages/index.php?art=694

another because our true reality or soul purpose says that *no Human being is an enemy of another Human being.*

We cannot be enemies of each other because our essential function or blueprint as a Human being is to *help not harm* one another which brings us to another great body of enlightened thought.

In Christianity, it is said that the way to God is through Jesus, and Jesus himself gave us the Two Great Commandments that contain the Whole Law of God which itself contains the direction that ALL Religions and moral philosophies take—for the right existence in the world:

> *"Then one of them, which was a lawyer, asked him a question, tempting him, and saying, Master, which is the great commandment in the law?*
>
> *Jesus said unto him,*
>
> *'Thou shalt love the Lord thy God with all thy heart, and with all thy soul, and with all thy mind.*
>
> *This is the first and great commandment. And the second is like unto it,*
>
> *Thou shalt love thy neighbor as thyself.*
>
> *On these two commandments hang all the law and the prophets.'"* [5]

---

[5] Matthew 22:35–40

With soul purpose or dharma, God is foremost in our world through the Oneness of life and our compassion and respect for it. As we exist in a sacred manner with our dharma or soul purpose we are caring, sharing, helping, saving and serving life, which at the same time is loving God with our whole being.

What greater purpose and truth is there in life than when all Religions and the great Ideals point to and agree with the inherent Equality in all? And thus, all are inherently deserving of Life, Liberty and Happiness as the right way to experience the world, through the right way to exist in the world—through our soul purpose or dharma which manifests our unique individuality in and *for* the world—*making all war obsolete.*

3 Joining Both Sides of the Divide: East Meets West and the Abolition of All War—The Five Fundamental Principles of the American Founding (West–1776 AD) Are Fundamental to Islam (East–610 AD)

> *The most formidable weapon against errors of every kind is reason.*
> — Thomas Paine

A Re-invigoration of Humanity into Religion and Nationality

ON THE BASIS OF OUR DHARMA or soul purpose, where we are helping all and harming none, Equality of all needs no war. Both America (West) and Islam (East) have their basis and First Principle in God, Whose Creation is the Equality of life itself where everything has a soul purpose for the unfolding and expanding of Creation. Dharma, as our true or spiritual path on the Planet, allows us a new orbit or dimension of energy that is not engaged in entropy—or death, decay and destruction.

In the Equality of life as recognition of God, all are made Whole through their fundamental essence or truth which is to help not harm—i.e. to be harmless as the way and the life on the Planet.

From the First Principle—God—all other universal principles and ideals parallel themselves in both the Founding of America in 1776 and in the great mission of the Prophet of Islam several hundred years after the birth of Christ when degradation, oppression and the loss of purpose was again bearing down on Humanity. On closer examination of the way of America and the way of Islam, we find there are no differences—where in fact the way of America has super-imposed itself on the way of Islam where *America is the New Islam.*

America's founding principles, universal ideals and soul or sacred purpose are seen through her Founding documents and all the rest of The People's sacred national inheritance which include:

The Declaration of Independence, the Constitution, the Bill of Rights, the Double Sided Seal, the Pledge of Allegiance and President Lincoln's Gettysburg Address.

The super-imposition and the parallels of the founding of America and Islam are as follows:

[1] First Principle in the Recognition of God and Equality of All:

America: *"We hold these truths to be self-evident, that all men are created equal, that they are endowed by their Creator with certain unalienable Rights, that among these are Life, Liberty, and the pursuit of Happiness."*

Islam: "The Prophet preached a message that was intensely democratic, insisting that in the sight of his Lord all people were equal."[6] The social content of his teachings brought social justice to an unjust order. Further, enforcement of the uniformity of thought was not considered God-centered or Islamic as the Prophet said, "Differences of opinion within my community is a sign of the bounty of Allah."[7]

From the First Principle—God—the four other Fundamental Principles flow for the Life, Liberty, Happiness and Progress of Humanity:

[2] E Pluribus Unum—"Out of Many, One" [Life Under God]:

America: Despite differing races, cultures, ethnicities, religions, intellectual differences, dispositions and social bearing of the person, there is one common thread that ties all people in together as one, and at the same time makes them unique. That quality is simply *respect*—through the recognition of the other's *self-worth*. All life is due respect because all life is Equal and thus equally worthy. Through respect for all and everything, *e pluribus unum* is fulfilled.

Islam: The Prophet himself recognized the innate living quality or core principle within all that transcended all differences when he invited a deputy of Christians visiting him to conduct their service in his mosque, adding,

---

[6] *The World's Religions: Our Great Wisdom Traditions*, Huston Smith (New York: HarperCollins, 1991), 227

[7] (ibid)

"It is a place consecrated to God."[8] The Prophet showed that respect to others is respect to God that goes beyond all differences.

[3] Religious Freedom and Free Speech:

America: All are free to worship and speak according to their own conscience with no authoritarian insistence or interference.

Islam: People were freed from their oppressors through the conquests of Islam which allowed all people in the conquered nations the freedom of worship in their own Religions which was contingent on a special tax in lieu of the Poor Due.[9] Thereafter, every interference with their liberty of conscience in the community was regarded as a direct contravention of Islam. Religious tolerance for all is at the heart of Islam by the Prophet's own words, "Will you then force men to believe when belief can come only from God?"[10]

[4] Protection of Individuality, the Common Good and Liberty:

America: A strong moral framework for responsibility, accountability, transparency, fairness and truth-telling allows the proper relationship between the government and the people as an untouchable

---

[8] (ibid), 256

[9] See the Islamic notion of zakāt or almsgiving Chapter 4, p. 35 and Chapter 9, p. 96

[10] *The World's Religions: Our Great Wisdom Traditions*, Huston Smith (New York: HarperCollins, 1991), 256

agreement between the two—with Militias (of the Second Amendment) being the backup to the agreement in the protection of the People's God-given rights from tyrannical government.

With the moral framework expressed in great documents such as the Bill of Rights and the Ten Commandments, governments cannot degenerate into tyranny, oppression, deception, secrecy and stupidity—or lying, cheating, thieving, stealing, oppressing and killing. At the same time, morally unrestrained and undisciplined individuals within society cannot continue to break the common good of the nation until there is no nation.

In a progressive society, the moral framework protects the interest of self, liberty and life where—in Abraham Lincoln's words, "touched by the better Angels of our nature"—the individual will be enhanced to the point where ultimately there is no need for government. The cultivation of morality and character is essential where the individual would be less dominated by his or her "animal" (lower or basal) nature, and more expressive of his or her own divine (higher or moral) nature. Our higher or divine nature would allow our moral autonomous (self-governing) selves to govern from within, making external government unnecessary and obsolete—as we follow the trajectory of the American Experiment to its conclusion:

I have no fear that the result of our experiment will be that men may be trusted to govern themselves without a master.
— Thomas Jefferson

Islam: The purpose of the moral framework of America parallels the notion of the "greater and lesser jihad" of Islam where it also refers to both the government and the individual. The Prophet discerned that the protection of the common good is within the bounds of the protection of the individual when he observed, back at his home base following an encounter with the tyrants, "We have returned from the lesser jihad [fight with the external enemy] to face the greater jihad [fight with the internal enemy]."[11] What this means is that the greater battle is not outside with one's enemies, but with the lesser being or the *oppressor* of one's higher or real Self within.

Jihad literally means "exertion." But exerting what?—exerting force to the good. The Quran says, "Turn away evil with that which is better" (42:37)—not only within oneself, but through the action of a government. Not only is the government to protect the framework of its core and guiding principles against those who seek to interfere and subvert it from within, but it is also to exert force through policy toward that which is better for the individual.

But who is to say what is good or what is better for the individual, the individual him- or herself or the government? Neither—it is simply the wisdom and morality of the principles that are to *lead* all from leaders to individuals. However, it is the leader—if we are to follow—who must grasp them more clearly and apply them more fully,

---

[11] (ibid), 257

which is the reason we have had great Prophets. The moral philosophers and all Religions, wisdom traditions and philosophies carry with them a great body of ethical and moral thought that allows us to be free of evil, temptations and enslavement by our personal appetites, misconceptions and deceptions (illusions and delusions) in both our personal and collective lives.

The great teachings say that freedom is not a material value, like being free to consume or buy things. It is an internal value of a transcendent knowledge and responsibility that has an ethical and moral quality (freedom with responsibility) that informs our being and shapes our behavior and, at the same time, engages our soul purpose. It is what Socrates meant when he said, "Virtue is knowledge." In short, virtue is a cultivation of our life as a straight ideal and character that motivates us to *always* put our best foot forward—without fail or compromise.

The great moral philosopher, Immanuel Kant said, "From the crooked timber of Humanity, no straight thing can be made." Thus we see, through the founding principles and ideals of America as they are superimposed on the fundamental principles of the Prophet's mission in Islam—as both emanate from God as a given unity or First Principle (of Equality)—we have the basis for good things to be made or a strong foundation to build Humanity and the world we have. At the same time, Islam is not simply a Religion, but—like America where America herself is the new Islam—a way for all to express a *unity in diversity* that enhances individuality:

> *"To every one have We given a law and a way.... And if God had pleased, he would have made [all humankind] one people [people of one religion]. But He hath done otherwise, that He might try you in that which He hath severally given unto you: wherefore press forward in good works. Unto God shall ye return, and He will tell you that concerning which ye disagree"* (5:48).[12]

Through both America and Islam, diversity is allowed to express itself in the best way and in a progressive way through a moral context, and at the same time, the Founders of America and the Quran itself has stated that the drive toward our moral fitness through diversity or different expressions of life is both a *test* and an *experiment* to reach our ultimate existence as a Humanity.

> *"But He [God] hath done otherwise [created different religions], that He might <u>try you</u> in that which He hath severally given unto you"* [emphasis added] (ibid).
>
> *I have no fear that the result of our <u>experiment</u> will be that men may be trusted to govern themselves without a master.* [emphasis added].
>
> — Thomas Jefferson

---

[12] (ibid), 255

The test and experiment is a work out and an expression of our moral existence through the Fifth Fundamental Pivotal Principle of both America and Islam: Money.

4 The Fifth Fundamental Pivotal Principle of Both America and Islam: Money Must Be Usury-Free

> *"Man is a rational animal, endowed by nature with rights and with an innate sense of justice."*
> — Thomas Jefferson

IN BOTH ETHICAL STRUCTURES of the Four Fundamental Principles of America and Islam we see—in the transcendence in the notion of any nationality—a fundamental morality that excludes them both from *any particular ethnocentricity* that would make them ethnically, racially or nationally oriented.

That fundamental morality manifests the reality for "a more perfect union" of Humanity—just as we find in the preamble to the American Constitution:

> *"We the People of the United States, in Order to form a more perfect Union, establish Justice, insure domestic Tranquility, provide for the common*

> *defense, promote the general Welfare, and secure the Blessings of Liberty to ourselves and our Posterity, do ordain and establish this Constitution for the United States of America."*

The formation of the more perfect union indeed brings forth blessings, and so to secure and expand on the work of the Four Fundamental Principles is the Fifth Fundamental Principle of both America and Islam, which like the first Four, is to reflect or obey the Will of God (to enjoy those blessings)—that being:

[5] Money Must be Usury-Free

America: The original and real cause of the American Revolution: money must be usury-free, i.e., no interest, debt or taxes involved in its printing and issuing. Money must not be a thing-in-itself or a product to be owned by anyone as an "us and them" system to take advantage of (i.e., enslave) others (i.e., the population) through debt and interest that presents itself as income tax on the population[13]—*it must simply facilitate Human life.* Money is to be like oil through an engine, and not be the engine itself.

The following historical story is taken from a radio address given by Congressman Charles G. Binderup of Nebraska, some 50 years ago and was reprinted in *Unrobing the Ghosts of Wall Street:*[14]

---

[13] See background of the printing and issuing of America's money: http://www.thespiritualun.org/federalreserve.htm

[14] Compiled by anon., see: http://www.biblebelievers.biz/debtmone.htm

Colonies More Prosperous Than the Home Country

Before the American War for Independence in 1776, the colonized part of what is today the United States of America was a possession of England. It was called New England, and was made up of 13 colonies, which became the first 13 states of the great Republic. Around 1750, this New England was very prosperous. Benjamin Franklin was able to write:

"There was abundance in the Colonies, and peace was reigning on every border. It was difficult, and even impossible, to find a happier and more prosperous nation on all the surface of the globe. Comfort was prevailing in every home. The people, in general, kept the highest moral standards, and education was widely spread."

When Benjamin Franklin went over to England to represent the interests of the Colonies, he saw a completely different situation: the working population of this country was gnawed by hunger and poverty. "The streets are covered with beggars and tramps," he wrote. He asked his English friends how England, with all its wealth, could have so much poverty among its working classes.

His friends replied that England was a prey to a terrible condition: it had too many workers!

The rich said they were already overburdened with taxes, and could not pay more to relieve the needs and poverty of this mass of workers. Several rich Englishmen of that time actually believed, along with Malthus, that wars and plague were necessary to rid the country from man-power surpluses.

Franklin's friends then asked him how the American Colonies managed to collect enough money to support their poor houses, and how they could overcome this plague of pauperism. Franklin replied:

"We have no poor houses in the Colonies; and if we had some, there would be nobody to put in them, since there is, in the Colonies, not a single unemployed person, neither beggars nor tramps."

Thanks To Free Money Issued By The Nation

His friends could not believe their ears, and even less understand this fact, since when the English poor houses and jails became too cluttered, England shipped these poor wretches and down-and-outs, like cattle, and discharged, on the quays of the Colonies, those who had survived the poverty, dirtiness and privations of the journey. At that time, England was throwing into jail those who could not pay their debts.

They therefore asked Franklin how he could explain the remarkable prosperity of the New England Colonies. Franklin replied:

"That is simple. In the Colonies, we issue our own paper money. It is called 'Colonial Scrip.' We issue it in proper proportion to make the goods pass easily from the producers to the consumers. In this manner, creating ourselves our own paper money, we control its purchasing power and we have no interest to pay to no one" [sic].

The Bankers Impose Poverty

The information came to the knowledge of the English Bankers, and held their attention. They immediately took the necessary steps to have the British Parliament to pass a law that prohibited the Colonies from using their scrip money, and then ordered them to use only the gold and silver money that was provided in sufficient quantity by the English bankers. Then began in America the plague of debt-money, which has ever since brought so many curses to the American people.

The first law was passed in 1751, and then completed by a more restrictive law in 1763. Franklin reported that one year after the implementation of this prohibition on Colonial money, the streets of the Colonies were filled with unemployment and beggars, just like in England, because there was not enough money to pay for the goods and work. The circulating medium of exchange had been reduced by half.

Franklin added that this was the original cause of the American Revolution—and not the tax on tea or the Stamp Act, as it has been taught again and again in history books. The financiers always manage to have removed from school books all that can throw light on their own schemes, and damage the glow that protects their power.

Franklin, who was one of the chief architects of American independence, wrote about it clearly:

"The Colonies would gladly have borne the little tax on tea and other matters had it not been the poverty caused by the bad influence of the English bankers on the Parliament, which has caused in the Colonies hatred of England and the Revolutionary War."

This point of view of Franklin was confirmed by great statesmen of his era: John Adams, Jefferson and several others. A remarkable English historian, John Twells, wrote, speaking of the money of the Colonies, the Colonial Scrip:

"It was the monetary system under which America's Colonies flourished to such an extent that Edmund

Burke was able to write about them: 'Nothing in the history of the world resembles their progress. It was a sound and beneficial system, and its effects led to the happiness of the people.'" John Twells adds:

"In a bad hour, the British Parliament took away from America its representative money, forbade any further issue of bills of credit, these bills ceasing to be legal tender, and ordered that all taxes should be paid in coins. Consider now the consequences: this restriction of the medium of exchange paralyzed all the industrial energies of the people. Ruin took place in these once flourishing Colonies; most rigorous distress visited every family and every business, discontent became desperation, and reached a point, to use the words of Dr. Johnson, when human nature rises up and asserts its rights."

Another writer, Peter Cooper, expresses himself along the same lines. After having said how Franklin had explained to the London Parliament the cause of the prosperity of the Colonies, he wrote:

"After Franklin gave explanations of the true cause of the prosperity of the Colonies, the Parliament exacted laws forbidding the use of this money in the payment of taxes. This decision brought so many drawbacks and so much poverty to the people that it was the main cause of the Revolution. The

> *suppression of the Colonial money was a much more important reason for the general uprising than the Tea and Stamp Act."*

Through the American pre-Revolutionary War experience, the issue of interest-free money that incurs no income taxes on the population is inextricably tied in with Happiness and the quality of life which is fundamental to the progress and uplift of Humanity. The God-inspired American Revolution of 1776 gave us a cornerstone and a pillar in regard to people and money:

Money must serve and facilitate Human purpose, and not the other way around. Money must not be a product or a thing-in-itself, it must simply be a way and means to facilitate Human industry through the releasing of Human creative energies and potential, which is vast—for *each and every Human being* carries a unique blueprint of their sacred or Divine purpose (dharma) on the Planet.

As money becomes simply the facilitator of the release of Human creative potential, the fruits of one's labor or the sweat of one's brow are no longer stolen through income taxes that are given to the usurers for the interest paid on debt money. At the same time, income taxes are a form of direct theft of life from the Human, and through the sweat of one's brow an enslavement of the very essence or being of a Human over the span of his or her life time. In other words, the fraudulent system of usury diminishes Human life and potential and thwarts, if not extinguishes, Human purpose at the same time.

Islam: Usury is a grave sin and offence in Islam. Two verses in the Quran strictly and sternly prohibit usury:

> *"Those who devour usury will not stand except as stand as one whom the Evil one by his touch hath driven to madness. That is because they say: 'Trade is like usury,' but God hath permitted trade and forbidden usury. Those who after receiving direction from their Lord, desist, shall be pardoned for the past; their case is for God [to judge]; but those who repeat [the offence] are companions of the Fire: They will abide therein [for ever]."* — Quran Verse 2:275 (Chapter Al-Baqara)

> *"O ye who believe! Fear God, and give up what remains of your demand for usury, if ye are indeed believers."* — Quran Verse 2:278 (Chapter Al-Baqara)

The verse, "if ye are indeed believers," further highlights the gravity of the offence by exhorting people to obey if they indeed call themselves people of God.

The Quran not only puts a stop on usury but it also encourages leniency toward the debt-ridden as a way to social upliftment.

> *"If the debtor is in a difficulty, grant him time Till it is easy for him to repay. But if ye remit it by way of charity (forgiveness of debt), that is best for you if ye only knew."* — Quran Verse 2:280 (Chapter Al-Baqara)

At the same time, what also would be an agreement with Islam in the freedom and social uplift of nations is an established international legal principle—odious debt or debt repudiation—where people do not have to repay their government's debt to the extent that it is incurred to launch aggressive wars or to oppress the people. Such debts are considered "odious," i.e., they are the personal debts of tyrants or the oppressors who incurred them and therefore they are neither the business nor the responsibility of the people.

The strict prohibition of usury or interest in Islam is a result of its deep concern for the economic, moral and social welfare of the people. The American pre-Revolutionary War experience depicts very well the self-explanatory reality of those factors that comprise the welfare and well being of the people and society as a whole:

> *"There was abundance in the Colonies, and peace was reigning on every border. It was difficult, and even impossible, to find a happier and more prosperous nation on all the surface of the globe. Comfort was prevailing in every home. The people,*

in general, kept the highest moral standards, and education was widely spread."

The only money required from the people in Islam is simply a small portion of the fruits of their labor to assist and uplift the poor, a portion which, on a collective level of the population, would be significant and adequate. It is called zakāt or almsgiving. For non-Muslims in the conquered nations of Islam, as they were freed from their oppressors and allowed freedom of worship, there was a special tax in lieu of the "Poor Due." With all people contributing to the poor, while at the same time developing a charitable and ethical heart of the government, there would be an inbuilt societal movement to progressing the poor and growing equality through the dissolution of class differences, which is paramount in Islam.

At the same time, in Christianity, there is an emphasis on the poor who are to be assisted, not so much through piecemeal charitable contributions, but more as a definite societal obligation for the rest of us—as a taking care of each other. The qualities that are to be instilled are mercy, kindness and concern for the poor, the weak, the oppressed and the outcast. Throughout the whole Bible, both the First and Second Testament, we are given an ethic for both social and economic justice, not just amongst one another as Human beings, but with the land itself—as a sacred relationship—where God is the owner and, consequently, in obedience to His way as the right way to exist on the Earth which secures both our safety and happiness.[15]

In the whole continuum of thought or ethic regarding our behavior through the three socio-historical, *Semite* religions of Judaism, Christianity and Islam, the Quran says:

> *"We made a covenant of old with the Children of Israel*[16] *[and] you have nothing of guidance until you [also] observe the Torah and the Gospel."* (5:70, 68).

---

[15] A concise reference to the relationship of God, Human beings and land as an ethical continuum is seen in the "Year of the Lord's favor," the year of jubilee: the time when land was given its rest, slaves were freed and debts were forgiven—Leviticus 25 and Luke 4: 14–21—which, in our modern world, would be the fair and equitable system doing away with the whole usurious system of war-debt-taxes, and by way of extension, Monolithic-Monopoly Business that is destroying all—see Chapters 6 and 9.

[16] As the Revelation of the Quran came to the Prophet Muhammad beginning 610 AD, "Israel" therefore does not at all involve the geographical location or the strife-ridden artificially and politically created state in the Middle East some 50 years or so ago. Instead, the name "Israel" concurs with the deeper or true meaning of a coming together of the totality of sacred people, i.e., people of God with a common interest to uphold the idealized society with having the effect of great happiness. ("The Meaning of the Name of Israel," Theodor H. Gaster review of "Studies in the Name Israel in the Old Testament," by G.A. Danell, *The Jewish Quarterly Review*, New Series, Vol. 37, No. 4 (Apr., 1947), pp. 425–426, University of Pennsylvania Press).

Further, Semite is not, and never is to be exclusive to simply any one of the three major Religions of Judaism, Christianity or Islam, but is inclusive of <u>all three</u> as the *obedience, faith* and *submission* to God that descended from the righteous forefather of all three—Abraham.

In other words, the body of the whole ethical thought that we find in Judaism, Christianity and Islam are to be incorporated in the Muslim's way of life where none of the Holy Books are exclusive of the other. At the same time, the Quran gives guidance and light to Jews and Christians to apply the same as all are of the "One" God, or the people of God or the *good* way.

Helping and uplifting the poor is paramount in all the Religions. No other system is required other than uplifting and helping each other and the poor as it serves the First Principle of Equality as a direct Law of God—where we find that *Equality needs no war.*

The binding unity through diversity is through the **Five Fundamental Principles** of both the American Founding and Islam, in obedience to the Will, Way or Law of God—i.e., in the context of the sacred relationship with the Earth that allows all of society to be progressive and free at the same time. The obedience to the right way is preliminary or prerequisite to Happiness *for all members* of the Human Race and is not restricted to race, color, creed, religion or ethnicity.

Thus we find, in the big picture, in the context of Human life and freedom, absent the good way or *God way* as universal, we have the reality of where one group or one individual is simply lording it over the others—which is retrogressive, stagnant and ultimately unacceptable to all people in the progress and *equality* of all Life.

5 How We Are to Flow Life, Liberty, Happiness and Right Progress of <u>All</u> of Humanity— Without Sin for Religious People, and Without Error for Rational People

> *The salvation of mankind lies only in making everything the concern of all.*
> — Alexander Solzhenitsyn

THE FIRST PRINCIPLE in the recognition of God is Equality—which enlightens us about our own Human Needs, and which agrees with the spiritual precepts in all Religions that in reality progress one and all at the same time. Fulfillment of our Human Needs is the true definition of world progress where technology itself would be brought into line to simply assist our own Human Needs, helping all and harming none, including all realms of life on the Planet as well as the integrity of the Earth itself. Through the Hopi Prophecy of the path of our self-annihilation through the violent and violate life, we have all the technology, through the system of War, to kill, harm and destroy each other and the Earth, but none to heal and help mankind and that is *at the same time* in harmony with all living systems.

To choose the true path of the gentle life, we must return ourselves to our God-given Humanity. To begin with, as fundamental to all, is the fulfillment of our basic and enhanced Human Needs that we find ordered in Maslow's hierarchical pyramid of needs.[17] Each level that is met enables us to grow and expand to the next level of Human existence as a Oneness of Life on the Planet—as God asks of us all through the spiritual path which essentially is the fulfilling path for *all* Humans.

Our existence therefore is simply:

Fulfilling our Fundamental Human Needs Through the Three Levels of Existence of the Body-Mind-Spirit Continuum of the Whole Human

The first and basic level of our collective Human Needs before we can progress to the second level of our existence are our body or physical needs which are:

1) *Clean Water, Food, Clothing, Shelter*

Without the fulfillment of these basic physical needs we cannot progress any further because we are constantly in our *survival mode*. However, when these are satisfied we

---

[17] An American psychologist (April 1, 1908–June 8, 1970)

are then ready to move to the second level of our Human Needs which is:

2) *Education*

When we are fed, watered and sheltered, so to speak, we are ready and able to progress further to our second level of our existence—which is the meeting of our mind needs.

Education is the instrument that opens our minds to feed the thought of our soul—to be able to think and question ideas, the world and ourselves. It allows us not only the "how," but also the "what" and the "why" of something. Education is a powerful tool to explore and open both hemispheres of the brain—the left and right, or the analytical and the creative, which are essential for a fully functioning mind and, thus, satisfying the second level of our basic Human Needs.

However, in Human existence and purpose, and beyond comfort and consumerism, mind needs are not enough to fulfill the Human spirit in a progressive and evolutionary way to find ultimate satisfaction, contentment and bliss. Human existence thus advances to the third level of existence.

3) *Self-Actualization*

Because the rational mind is not enough to complete knowledge, we have the drive to a higher aspect of ourselves for fulfillment—our spiritual need—which takes care of our whole being or *wholeness*.

Our spiritual need is grasped through the Realm of the Good, True, Beautiful and Right—a realm of Wholeness—beyond the physical. It is the Realm of Ideals or the Platonic Forms where Reality can be fitted into one over-arching conceptual scheme that brooks no contradiction.

For example, we can grasp the idea of the Good, True, Beautiful and Right through the following reply by Will Campbell[18] on the notion of capital punishment, which he thought was tacky:

> *"Yessir [to the moderator]. I know what it means [the word 'tacky'—an old Southern word that means 'uncouth,' 'ugly,' 'lack of class']. And if a thing is ugly, well, ugly means there's no beauty there. And if there is no beauty in it, there is no truth in it. And if there is no truth in it, there is no good in it. Not for the victim of the crime. Certainly not for the one being executed. Not for the executioner, the jury, the judge, the state. For no one. And we were enjoined by a well known Jewish prophet to love them all."*

The realm of Wholeness is exactly that, it is all—a transcendent ethic and knowledge combined through (our)

---

[18] Will Campbell has been a Baptist preacher, civil rights activist, farmer, writer, and volunteer cook for his friend, Waylon Jennings. Quoted in "Soul of a Citizen, Living with Conviction in a Cynical Time," by Paul Rogat Loeb, Utne Reader, July–August, 1999, p. 52

virtue—as Socrates said, "virtue is knowledge." Virtue is a behavior that aligns us to the Realm of Wholeness and Knowledge *already within ourselves* which fulfills our being with enlightenment and bliss.[19] Because the Good, True, Beautiful and Right is a whole ethic, indivisible, where each is the other, existing through the realm of Wholeness, it harms none and advances all—it is the right way, and the right existence for Humans as we at the same time meet and complete ourselves through our spiritual need.[20]

Further, Einstein said:

> *"The intuitive mind is a sacred gift and the rational mind is a faithful servant. We have created a society that honors the servant and has forgotten the gift."*

The intuitive mind, along with insights and inspirations, is the meeting point of mind and Spirit, the realm of genius, creativity, ethic and morality all combined. And since it is a sacred point of the meeting of mind

---

[19] Enlightenment and bliss (and the gentle state of the Earth) is a palpable state of the transcendent **knowledge within** and is described through Nature in Isaiah 11:9: "They shall not hurt nor destroy in all my holy mountain: for the earth shall be full of the knowledge of the LORD, as the waters cover the sea" and "The wolf and the lamb shall feed together, and the lion shall eat straw like the bullock: and dust [shall be] the serpent's meat. They shall not hurt nor destroy in all my holy mountain, saith the LORD." — Isaiah 65:25

[20] The spiritual need of the transcendent realm of the Whole ethic is facilitated through the "going within" through the practice of meditation.

and Spirit, it is an inviolate expression of Love beyond the rational mind's faculties of thinking and logic. At the same time we find, in Pierre Teilhard de Chardin's visionary thought of the future of Man:

> *"Love is the affinity which links and draws together the elements of the world . . . Love, in fact, is the agent of universal synthesis."*

Our rational mind is our incomplete mind with a limited effect in our world and in our being. Love (mind + Spirit), on the other hand, is the glue of the world, i.e., the universe itself that fulfills our whole being in the body-mind-*spirit* continuum as it naturally includes the heart (the affinity and the agent of fulfillment). It completes us and moves us to greater heights of being and living. It is here we become self-actualized, and it is in this disposition of being we are also in the realm of *agape* or brotherly love—our love for one another and mankind—where the personal becomes the universal, i.e., our thoughts and actions in alignment with heart are in harmony with all and everything, the whole continuum of life, meaning *no harm*.

"No harm" is of course the realm of our dharma, without the karma, and so through the Third Level of Human Existence as we are experiencing the personal, we are also naturally in our dharma, the universal way of being.

Thus, through the Third Level of Human Existence, by way of the meeting of mind and Spirit in each and every *Human mind and heart,* is the unique blueprint we all carry as to our true purpose on Earth as simply individuals in harmony with all. Our soul purpose or dharma is to give to and grow the Whole (Self + world) in our own unique way that fulfills and satisfies our own being and at the same time the world's. It is the highest level of our existence, an expansion into our full creative potential as Human beings where the possibilities as co-creators (self + Spirit)—i.e., with the Creator through the Realm of Wholeness (that we know as the Good, True, Beautiful and Right)—are exhilarating.

In the spiritual-religious sense, self-actualizing our full creative potential is an elevating dialogue *and creative relationship* with the universal God.

Without the fulfillment and opening to our spiritual need, we can exist simply in the rational mind, but as we find in Jungian psychology, an over preponderance of the rational mind will flip the mind poles of opposites to the *irrational*—the experience of life that moves us out of the virtues and into harm's way through the cycle of entropy, degeneration, decay and all the addictions. It is the reason why the moral philosophers gave us the notion of "care of the soul" and why we cannot do without ethics and morality if we are to advance ourselves and the world.

At the same time, the *over preponderance* of the rational mind over the Reality and Truth of the existence of God is the static state and has all the worth of a broken record—with the same tune or line played over and over. It is the "unreflective life" which Socrates said "is not worth living" and which, in material reality, is the same as entropy.

Taking the Spiritual Path of the Hopi Prophecy for Our Continued Existence and Future on the Planet

Satisfying the fundamental needs of our body-mind-spirit through the Three Levels of Existence has a very real and tangible effect on the world and is further laid out simply through **Five Universal Mandates** as the basis of a moral and Humane existence for all Humanity—in contrast and in the transcendence of any ideology and War itself—because it is simply about the Human being.

The **Five Universal Mandates** for a Planet-wide re-design in the free movement of all is simply the fulfillment of our Human Needs in the drive to our unique individuality which through the ethic of Wholeness, harms none and helps all—matching the Creator's perfect Design for evolution and Life.

The ethic of Wholeness is not about rules, laws and regulations—upon more rules, laws and regulations. It is simply a way on the Planet that harms none and advances all through the concept of "Holistic," i.e., "no rules, just right" through the Good, True, Beautiful and Right which brooks no contradictions.

"The Whole" has the moral dimension of (W)Holy or Sacred which distills itself into the Human disposition of *Respect* (for all and everything) which engenders "No Harm," for we find in all spiritual traditions and even in the science of the quantum (quantum physics) that we are all *One Life,* or as in Genesis, "One Blood" after all (1:26–28).

"Holistic" is from the ancient Greek word "Holism" meaning "all," "entire," "total." In other words, what is good for Humans is good for the Animals is good for the Environment as One Seamless Whole.

Holistic, in the ethic of Wholeness, thus means, regarding "the Whole," *without harm.* Translated on a Planet-wide basis it would not only be a humane *and intact* Planet for all life—human, animal, plant and mineral—but it would also be a toxic-free Planet, i.e., a Planet with no toxins which immediately eliminates all war and weaponry and allows us all to cross over to the *spiritual path of the Hopi Prophecy of peace and plenty for all* for our continued existence and future on the Planet as a Human or *humane* species.

In the Hopi language, the word *Koyaanisqatsi* means "crazy life, life in turmoil, life out of balance, life disintegrating, a state of life that calls for another way of living." Living in balance through the ethic of Wholeness means we will be treading gently on the Earth with no need to violate any of the Earth's vast systems that keep the Planet intact and in its integrity and balance. The concept of "holistic" in the ethic of Wholeness draws on our full creative potential and genius to create without harm, while at the same time developing our full creative potential and genius *of, by and for all* as a truly deeply and deepening democratic experience.

The ethic of Wholeness in the Oneness of Life is our true **world purpose** on the Planet and is captured *simply* in **Five Universal Mandates** which, at the same time, fulfill all our Human Needs planet-wide. No longer are we deceived by the false reality of the "balance of weapons" and the need for war, but now free to experience our *true reality* through the **balance of the heart**—where all is in perfect balance with the Earth and the progress of all. Simply, and spiritually, it is where our heart song meets Earth song as the good stewardship and caring for all people and life on the Planet.

6 Putting Money to Work for the Good Stewardship and Caring for the Planet and All People

> *It is the criterion of a just money system that what is both socially and physically possible should also be made financially possible.*
> — Eric Encina

THE FIVE UNIVERSAL MANDATES for the complete advancement of Man and the Planet are:

1. *Clean Water, Clean Air, Clean Soil and Clean Seas through Holistic Farming, Holistic Industry and Holistic Science*

2. *The Trend Toward a Vegetarian Diet, a Powerful and Balanced Immune System through Holistic Medicine, and New Regard for Animal Life*

3. *The Finest and Best Education through "Whole" Education Freely Available through Free Government Funding, and Freely Accessible Through Merit (Performance) and Opportunity*

4. *Prisons as Teaching/Learning Centers*

5. *Welfare Housing as Learning Communities (Learning to be a Community) for Those Who Cannot Yet Help Themselves*

Our whole Holistic structure exists on the spiritual pathway of the Hopi Prophecy that travels the path for our continued existence and future on the Planet. It is the path of the Promise of the Creator, of peace and plenty for all through the joining of the two tablets or the two types of knowledge, the ancient and the modern.

In the joining of the ancient and modern knowledge, we as a Humanity exist in an ethical and Holistic way that harms none and advances all. Through it, we use our God-given energies, talents, creativity and effort, or *our soul purpose or dharma,* to uplift all in fulfilling the needs of all Human beings and the world as we at the same time fulfill ourselves. To choose the spiritual path that serves God is to choose life and not the ruinous end of the world which is serving money or Mammon[21] in a world built for war, debt and usury that gives way to destructive war, greed and technology. Indeed, Will Rogers said:

> *"You can't say civilization doesn't advance, however, for in every war they kill you in a new way."*

---

[21] "Mammon" is the Aramaic word for money.

Militarism and war are a collective cancer that feeds on society and with every thinking and spiritually connected person we find it a total abomination on life itself that sums itself up as:

> *Waste of muscle, waste of brain: Waste of patience, waste of pain: Waste of work, waste of wealth: Waste of beauty, waste of health: Waste of blood and waste of tears: Waste of youth's most precious years: Waste of ways the saints have trod: Waste of glory, waste of GOD.*
> — Geoffrey Anketell Studdert Kennedy[22]

War and militarism are a central, TOXIC reality on the Planet that cannot be ignored and must, in the crossroads of our common future on the Planet, be decisively voted down by all People for the pro-Human way of life on the Planet.

Comprehending the Pro-Human Way of Life on the Planet by Way of the Five Universal Mandates

We are able to fulfill the fundamental Human Needs of the First Level of Existence (in Maslow's hierarchical pyramid of needs) of *clean water, food, clothing and shelter for all* through **Universal Mandate One:**

---

[22] Geoffrey Anketell Studdert Kennedy, (June 27, 1883–March 8, 1929), an Anglican priest and poet, nicknamed 'Woodbine Willie' during World War I. See:
http://en.wikipedia.org/wiki/Geoffrey_Anketell_Studdert_Kennedy

1. ***Clean Water, Clean Air, Clean Soil and Clean Seas through Holistic Farming, Holistic Industry and Holistic Science***

Through Universal Mandate One we are using and creating non-toxic, natural solutions and technology that is in harmony with all living systems on the Planet.

"Natural" means that we are no longer breaching the Planetary systems above and below the ground and are instead putting in place or inventing the ways that are good to all and that at the same time advance all without harm or destruction. When we travel the wrong path, without the joining of the two types of knowledge, the ancient and the modern, bad things happen.

For example, the Amazonian Indians of South America have said:

"The tropical rain forests support the sky—cut down the trees and disaster will follow."

The same with below the ground. The Hopi Indians have said:

"If we dig precious things from the land we will perish."

Natural also means the relinquishing of all chemicals and letting Nature provide for us as we follow Nature's ethic and natural systems. The Bible tells us:

> *"Six years thou shalt sow thy land, and shalt gather in the fruits thereof: But the seventh year thou shalt let it rest and lie still."* (Exodus 23:10–11)

and:

> *"When ye reap the harvest of your land, thou shalt not wholly reap the corners of thy field, neither shalt thou gather the gleanings of thy harvest."* (Leviticus 19:9)

In our modern world, soil is misused and abused in the way food is grown, which results in both soil erosion and very little nutritional value for the health of any living system. Dr. William A. Albrecht, Chairman of the Department of Soils at the University of Missouri, said:

> *"A declining soil fertility, due to a lack of organic material, major elements, and trace minerals, is responsible for poor crops and in turn for pathological conditions in animals fed deficient foods from such soils, and that mankind is no exception."*

Through the use of fertilizers and pesticides, and not the natural processes, problems compound until all life systems go out of balance. The enforced use of chemicals, including genetically modified seeds to grow our food, means:

"... malnutrition, attack by insects, bacteria and fungi, weed takeover, crop loss in dry weather, and general loss of mental acuity in the population, leading to degenerative metabolic disease and early death."[23]

Fertilizers cause mineral depletion and weaken the crop which in turn makes it more subject to insects, and with the application of pesticides, Dr. Jerome Weisner, Science Councillor to John F. Kennedy, stated way back in 1963 that "the use of pesticides is more dangerous than atomic fallout."

Further, Amerige Mosca, Italian scientist and winner of the Science Prize at the Brussels World Fair in 1958, said,

> "The damage resulting from nuclear radiation is the same as the damage resulting from the use of toxic genetic chemicals. The use of fungicides of organic syntheses annually causes the same damage to present and future generations as atomic fallout from 14,500 atomic bombs of the Hiroshima type (approximately 29 14-megaton hydrogen bombs)."

---

[23] Dr. William A. Albrecht, Soil Depletion: http://www.604industries.com/portal.php?page=58

The Good Stewardship and Caring for the Planet and All People

The elimination of all toxins and chemicals and returning the Earth to its natural systems and processes with respect for the Earth is the right way to exist on the Earth—physically, mentally and spiritually—for Human health, the health of the Planet *and the life and progress of both* are inextricably tied into each other:

> *When health is absent, wisdom cannot reveal itself, art cannot become manifest, strength cannot be exerted, wealth is useless, and reason is powerless*
> — Herophiles, 300 BC

If the Planet is not healthy, Humans cannot be healthy. The Planet must simply "be," "without added" anything.

We do not need chemicals of any sort, nor tampering when we have Nature for all our needs. "Mother" Nature provides for us—perfectly and abundantly when we work in respect, ethic and harmony with all of her systems and natural laws from the macrocosm to the microcosm, which brings us to **Universal Mandate Two:**

2. *The Trend Toward a Vegetarian Diet, a Powerful and Balanced Immune System through Holistic Medicine, and New Regard for Animal Life*

Holistic medicine, like our outer environment, is simply the return to the natural processes of our own body to maintain health and vitality—and there are many avenues of knowledge through the natural or holistic sciences and alternative medicine that we are able to learn, draw from and apply.

Pharmaceutical drugs on the other hand, like chemicals, fertilizers, pesticides and genetically engineered seeds and organisms are simply the creation of greed-driven people to own people's lives simply for profit:

> *"Since the marketplace for the pharmaceutical investment business depends upon the continued existence of diseases, the drugs it developed <u>were not intended to prevent, cure or eradicate disease</u> [emphasis added]. Thus, the goal of the global strategy was to <u>monopolize</u> health [emphasis added] for billions of people, with pills that [merely] cover symptoms but hardly ever address the root cause of disease. The deprivation of billions of people from having access to life saving information about the health benefits of natural health approaches, whilst at the same time establishing a monopoly with largely ineffective and frequently toxic patented drugs, caused disease and death in genocidal proportions.*
>
> *"This epidemic of unnecessary disability and death by the pharmaceutical business with disease is unparalleled in history."*[24]

---

[24] "The History of the Pharma Cartel" by Dr. Rath Health Foundation, http://www4.dr-rath-foundation.org/THE_FOUNDATION/history_of_the_pharma_cartel.html

And of course, the same can be said about the agricultural business through the use of pesticides, fertilizers and genetically modified organisms.[25]

On the spiritual path of the Hopi Prophecy for our continued existence and future on the Planet, the choice becomes being motivated by Monolithic-Monopoly Business or by the Planetary Consciousness. The Planetary Consciousness sees us all as an interconnected Whole, where harm to one—human-animal-plant-mineral—is harm to all and therefore must be creatively resolved in consciousness of the Whole as each element and life in Nature has a meaningful part to play in the purpose of Creation and evolution and the consequent upward momentum of the Planet.

Monolithic-Monopoly Business instead sees all life as "things" to be used and abused and put to death through its ways and its processes—which is the reason why not only violence (War) but cruelty itself has also been institutionalized.

Gandhi said, "You can judge the moral fiber of a nation by the way it treats its animals"; or we can just as well say, "We can judge the Humanity of ourselves by the way *we* treat our animals" through factory farming, animal research, shark finning and the like. Monolithic-Monopoly Business develops our appetites to over-consume and lose

---

[25] See also the myriad commercial uses of hemp, the Earth's own wonder plant of the Planet which has been suppressed by the same Monolithic-Monopoly Business forces of tyranny on the Planet: "The Marijuana Conspiracy: The Reason Hemp Is Illegal," by Doug Yurchey: http://www.lewrockwell.com/spl2/reason-hemp-is-illegal.html

our Humanity as a Race, and in so doing, we over-consume the Planet where, literally, we are eating ourselves out of house and home and destroying the planetary systems.

For example, we find that cattle consume 16 times as much grain as they produce as meat, and drink 5,124 gallons of water to produce a single pound of beef. The Hindus have it right when they said the cow is for other (sacred) purposes and for what it is capable of producing naturally and abundantly with its multiple products of raw milk, yogurt, cheese, butter and ghee.

In the larger picture we find:

> *"Livestock are responsible for 18 percent of the greenhouse gases that cause global warming, more than cars, planes and all other forms of transport put together; require 94 percent more land than growing crops; eat 70 percent of all the grain we produce [in the U.S.] and are food factories in reverse."*[26]

And,

> *"... Manure still escapes into streams and groundwater, sometimes leading to dramatic fish kills such as the 2005 spill into New York's Black River and the 1995 spill into North Carolina's New River Basin. Lester R. Brown's book* **Plan B 3.0** *(W. W. Norton) reports that we currently feed livestock*

---

[26] "Vegetarianism and the Environment," http://michaelbluejay.com/veg/environment.html

> *37 percent of the grain produced on the planet. Of the pesticides used to help grow these crops, the USDA estimates that five percent will wash off farmland and enter the water supply. These practices ensure that our water supply will remain at risk of contamination from a number of sources."*[27]

Further,

> *"...Antibiotics, pesticides and artificial hormones are becoming more prevalent in our food and water supply. A recent report commissioned by the Breast Cancer Fund, 'The Falling Age of Puberty in U.S. Girls: What We Know, What We Need to Know' by Sandra Steingraber, considers early puberty to be at least in part an <u>ecological disorder</u>"* [emphasis added].[28]

On top of all the internal and external harm produced from livestock raised for consumption we find waterways ruined by run-off and massive rainforest deforestation—all an endless and irreversible cycle of destruction until we have an intervention through Universal Mandate 2.

The trend toward a vegetarian diet and a new regard for animal life, in Universal Mandate 2—whether one meatless day a week or as a lifestyle choice—will return us

---

[27] "Environmental Facts and Statistics About Industrialized Animal Farms," http://www.upc-online.org/environment/70208facts.html

[28] "Before They're Ready," Your Health, March/April 2008, (ibid)

to a planetary, and at the same time, *Humane* consciousness necessary for the Planetary balance. We find there is enough food (and health) on the Planet for everyone if we let Nature work, without our interfering, *destructive, toxic and polluting* footprint and harm, by eliminating all artificially manufactured chemicals, organisms and Monolithic-Monopoly Business itself that pushes poison and destroys all our natural systems internally and externally—faster, bigger and more efficiently.[29]

In a return to Life, Liberty and Happiness on the Planet for all, a Planetary Consciousness has a relationship with God, as God teaches knowledge through Nature:

> *"But ask the animals, and they will teach you; or birds of the air and they will tell you; or speak to the earth and it will teach you; or let the fish of the sea inform you."* (Job 12:7–10)

There is much to be gained, a whole new world indeed in the simple word of "Respect" for *all life* on the Planet—bringing us to the last three remaining Universal Mandates for the advancement of Man and the Planet.

As we have fulfilled the fundamental Human Needs of the First Level of Existence (in Maslow's hierarchical pyramid of needs) of ***clean water, food, clothing and shelter***

---

[29] See the prime example of what a Monolithic-Monopoly Business is which operates out of all the parameters of health, common sense, ethic, morality, decency and democracy: http://www.thepeoplesvoice.org/cgi-bin/blogs/voices.php/2007/03/22/the_silent_war_on_the_people_of_india

for all through Universal Mandates 1 and 2, we are able to progress and fulfill the fundamental Human Needs of the Second and Third Levels of Human Existence (in Maslow's hierarchical pyramid of needs) of **Education** and **Self-Actualization** through the last three Universal Mandates:

3. *The Finest and Best Education through "Whole" Education Freely Available through Free Government Funding, and Freely Accessible through Merit (Performance) and Opportunity*

4. *Prisons as Teaching/Learning Centers*

5. *Welfare Housing as Learning Communities (Learning to be a Community) for Those Who Cannot Yet Help Themselves*

Education meets the mind needs of the Human being, which allows consciousness to move from the physical level of Human existence to the intellectual and creative levels of existence. Movement in this direction is a natural process of population self-regulation as physical energies are now harnessed for intellectual pursuits—with the real effects of a reduced population explosion on the Planet.[30]

In our ever-present dismal world, global facts tell us that 80 percent of the world's population live on less than $10.00 a day,[31] which means in reality they are lacking the

---

[30] "The Effect of Female Education on Fertility: A Simple Explanation," Anrudh K. Jain, The Population Council, New York, New York 10017, http://www.jstor.org/pss/2060948

[31] http://www.globalissues.org/article/26/poverty-facts-and-stats

basic needs of clean water (as it includes sanitation), food, clothing, shelter and education. It is clear no significant progress has been made to make it a better world for all through the organizing principle of profit and War[32]—when all the Prophets of God have asked us to go the other way—the spiritual way—of Love, which is the upliftment and betterment of all with the effect of peace and plenty for all as we are foretold in the Hopi Prophecy.

Movement in the upward direction of our collective existence means that Human learning is not simply the "how" of something, i.e., the knowledge of skills and mechanical techniques, or even the knowledge that fills libraries. These are just "half" an education. The "Whole" education gives the grounding of the "what" and "why" of the Human being. It is the philosophical ("the love of wisdom") and scientific ("the validation") process together that answers and gives satisfaction to the eternal question of the purpose of the Human being on Earth by what we know as the Socratic ideal of "Know Thyself."

A Whole education means to know and study the depth of ourselves through the **body-mind-spirit continuum** as both a person and a Human species so that we don't exist simply as a cog in a big machine that external forces are able to turn off and on at will, but to comprehend ourselves fully through the knowledge and laws of

---

[32] "Less than one percent of what the world spent every year on weapons was needed to put every child into school by the year 2000 and yet it didn't happen." (ibid)

our existence that are beyond the material, so that we are truly free to be all that we can be.[33]

As we incorporate higher, or *whole knowledge* into our learning we will naturally progress to the fundamental Human need of Self Actualization as the final, but open-ended and ever-expanding Third Level of Human existence of the inviolate expression of Love that engages our whole being—body-mind-spirit—through Wholeness, i.e. the Oneness of all life *everywhere*.

At the same time, the happiness of the individual is not simply about himself or herself, just as society is not about itself, which brings us to the fullness and wholeness (wholesomeness) of society itself with the inclusion of people in prisons and welfare housing through Universal Mandates 4 and 5:

4. *Prisons as Teaching/Learning Centers*

5. *Welfare Housing as Learning Communities (Learning to be a Community) for Those Who Cannot Yet Help Themselves*

Joseph Campbell[34] said:

---

[33] For an example of what *Whole education* would look like, see "The Science of Man" at the University of Science and Philosophy: http://www.philosophy.org

[34] Joseph Campbell (March 26, 1904–October 30, 1987), an American mythologist, writer and lecturer best known for his work in comparative mythology and comparative religion. His work is vast, covering many aspects of human experience. His philosophy is often summarized by his phrase, 'Follow your bliss,' http://en.wikipedia.org/wiki/Joseph_campbell

> *"Man should not be in service of society, society should be in service of Man"*

which means our societal structures must also serve or contribute to Human beings' advancement and enlightenment—no matter how fallen they may be—as in our interconnected Reality *what affects one, affects us all.*

In the Planetary Consciousness where we help, not harm any life anywhere, people need the opportunity of assistance in the hand-up[35] and not, simply we find, in the hand-out.

For society to keep moving in an upward direction where there is no stagnation for people, whether in prisons or welfare housing, opportunities must be inherent and present to aid the individual to become Whole, self-sufficient and all ultimately autonomous Human beings. Martin Luther King said,

> *"When people are placed in darkness, crimes will be committed, the guilty are not just those who commit the crimes but those who create the darkness."*

---

[35] The dynamic and creative energy of the Planetary Consciousness (through our Holistic World Planetary Paradigm) is fulfilling the opportunity of everyone, everywhere (in our rightful free movement on our naturally borderless Planet) giving to "the other" through what their unique being (i.e. their dharma) has to offer for the other's progress, benefit, boost, upliftment and enlightenment.

Through Universal Mandates 1–5, we have a whole and wholesome structure that enlightens every Human being in every facet of life to create an evolution out of the trap and depression of materiality's destruction, despair, division (politics), ignorance and tyranny, and opens the door to the Oneness of Life and its higher Realities of Love, Learning and Enlightenment that has us *all* in mind.

On the spiritual path of our Planetary Consciousness, as *we choose perpetual peace* over perpetual war, we know there is no longer the world of politics and profit at the expense of everyone and everything, but simply the pure joy of being alive with life in the discovery of the depth, knowledge and possibilities of the Human soul—*of all*—making and *healing the world Whole.*

7 Life, Liberty and Happiness— Money as Creative Oil

> *Why waste Humanity by subjecting it to poverty? Think of the difference that could be made if all of Humanity was allowed to flourish individually and collectively; think of all the ideas, art, expression, intellect and beauty we aren't getting from those who have no voice.*
> — Andrew Gavin Marshall

OUR LIFE, LIBERTY AND HAPPINESS is sourced naturally in our Truth that we are beings (of Love) that are designed to "help not harm" life (our dharma). Choosing the path of peace not war collectively puts us on the spiritual path of the Hopi Prophecy—out of technological and catastrophic destruction.

As we transfer our collective effort from War to Peace we halt the entropy of our world—the doom and destruction with all its calamities and attendant effects of pain, suffering, dissolution and despair.

War, we find, is the wrong fit for the Human soul because we are not designed to kill one another but to simply "love one another"—as the Great Commandment says—realigning us back to our Human soul.

When we look beyond fallacies and unexamined thought we find East meets West, or Islam meets America, in the First Principle of God and the Equality of All—for Equality needs no War in the dissolution of usury. The American Revolutionary War was the product of the disturbance of life, liberty and happiness through the imposition of debt money by the British bankers in the suppression of colonial money. The effect was and is always widespread unemployment, beggars and poverty, creating the class differences and the subsequent rift in Humanity's progress *together*.

Islam states that usury or debt money is strictly forbidden as it is deeply concerned with the economic, moral and social welfare of the people. Through the **Five Fundamental Principles**, found not only in the Prophet's mission in Islam but also in the Founding of America,[36] we have the guide and the parameters for the ideal existence that was America's pre-Revolutionary War experience:

> *There was abundance in the Colonies, and peace was reigning on every border. It was difficult, and even impossible, to find a happier and more prosperous nation*

---

[36] [1] Recognition of God and Equality of All
 [2] E Pluribus Unum—"Out of Many, One [Life Under God]"
 [3] Religious Freedom and Free Speech
 [4] Protection of Individuality, the Common Good and Liberty
 [5] Money Must be Usury-Free

> on all the surface of the globe. Comfort was prevailing in every home. The people, in general, kept the highest moral standards, and education was widely spread.
> — Benjamin Franklin[37]

Through the experience of Colonial Scrip in the Colonies we find:

> "... *We issue our own paper money. It is called 'Colonial Scrip.' We issue it in proper proportion to make the goods pass easily from the producers to the consumers. In this manner, creating ourselves our own paper money, we control its purchasing power and we have no interest to pay to no one.*"[38]

From the American pre-Revolutionary War experience we see that serving God and serving Mammon[39] produces two different worlds.

In the American pre-Revolutionary War experience money is simply the **Creative Oil** for the engine of Human creativity and nothing else. It is not a thing in itself, carrying any intrinsic value—it is not a commodity to be bought and sold and to govern the lives and livelihoods of Humans so as to become the machine itself. Such a world had been imposed by the British bankers on the

---

[37] See Chapter 4, footnote 14
[38] (ibid)
[39] "Mammon" is the Aramaic word for money, as mentioned previously.

Americans destroying their lives, liberty and happiness and was to be unacceptable.

Serving Mammon or money is the world of Usury, Debt and War and all its attendant atrocities on people and the Planet. It turns our world upside down and our values inside out and back to front, where money becomes God and people are things in service to it or whoever owns it.

Creating a World of Respect for All Life

Turning our world right side up means serving God, where Money is the **Creative Oil** we use to fulfill our **Fundamental Human Needs**[40] as we help, heal, save and redeem through the **Five Universal Mandates**[41] that at the same time unlock the full creative potential, compassion, Humanity and genius of all Human beings, *everywhere*. The way of Life in serving God

---

[40] 1) Clean water, Food, Clothing, Shelter
   2) Education
   3) Self-Actualization

[41] 1. Clean Water, Clean Air, Clean Soil and Clean Seas Through Holistic Farming, Holistic Industry and Holistic Science

2. The Trend Toward a Vegetarian Diet, a Powerful and Balanced Immune System through Holistic Medicine, and New Regard for Animal Life

3. The Finest and Best Education through "Whole" Education Freely Available through Free Government Funding, and Freely Accessible through Merit (Performance) and Opportunity

4. Prisons as Teaching/Learning Centers

5. Welfare Housing as Learning Communities (Learning to be a Community) for Those Who Cannot Yet Help Themselves

fulfills all as we ourselves become fulfilled through the ethic and path of the **Good, True, Beautiful and Right** where there are no need for laws upon laws because everything is just right—in balance—the way Nature and God created it; as the American Declaration of Independence puts it:

> *"We hold these truths to be self-evident, that all men are created equal, that they are endowed by their Creator with certain unalienable Rights, that among these are Life, Liberty, and the pursuit of Happiness."*

In our Holistic ethic of helping all and harming none we are "One Life" (as we know in quantum physics) or "One Blood" as we are informed in Genesis (1:26–28) to *begin again* anew, from a new place and a new consciousness where science meets Religion in the sacred, and both are discovering life through the other:

> *Religion without science is blind and science without religion is lame.*
> — Albert Einstein

And, at the same time, Einstein said:

> *No problem can be solved from the same level of consciousness that created it.*

In our choice to serve God, not Mammon—and we cannot serve both as both produce different worlds—we have moved as a collective from the War effort to the Peace effort, i.e., from dooming ourselves in entropy to the flowering of our full potential in design (dharma)—the *higher level* of consciousness and being in our world.

Choosing the spiritual path of the Hopi Prophecy for our continued existence and future on the Planet,[42] we are finally seeing the beautiful creations that we are as the **Five Universal Mandates** manifest themselves as the Sacred Circle of our meeting of the Human spirit with the Creator.

God's Promise of peace, plenty and blessings *for all* is now our reality on the Planet as we have begun, afresh and new on *the spiritual path* through the chalice of The Spiritual UN. Through it, we are able to turn our sights toward the higher world reality of Love, Light and Learning that engenders the Peace, Happiness, Upliftment and Equality of All—which all Human beings everywhere naturally desire.

---

[42] The Hopi Prophecy reveals two pathways or choices for Humanity on the Planet: *The great Spirit or Creator meets man. The Creator then gave man the Sacred Circle, a promised life of peace and plenty if, and only if, man would follow the spiritual path*—and not War and the subsequent destructive technology for power and control over all, including the natural Earth itself, which leads to catastrophic and total destruction.

8 Love's Turn on the Planet— Thomas Jefferson's "Governing Ourselves without a Master" and the Advancement of All

Human Nature is not meant to be 'controlled,' but rather is meant to be nurtured.
— Andrew Gavin Marshall

JUST AS THE FUNDAMENTAL HUMAN NEEDS of all Human beings are the same, i.e. *universal*, so are the grand principles we find in both America and Islam that engender a Brotherhood of Man.

In serving God in the Brotherhood of Equality we are fulfilling our fundamental Human Needs. In this new peaceful and joyful new world paradigm for Humanity we are in our right fit or function, and all problems come into balance both globally and nationally at the same time. For example, just as population explosion is the effect of the failure of the fulfilling of our fundamental Human Needs, so is mass immigration, for all people everywhere would . . .

> "... *prefer to stay at home with their families and live their own culture, eat their own food and listen to their own music.*"[43]

How to care for the Planet and Humanity as one seamless Whole requires neither master nor politician, for one requires slaves and the other nonsense bureaucracies.

The Equality of All is an ethical framework simple and free, allowing all to breathe the experience of Life, Liberty and Happiness undisturbed by any tyranny.

Laying it all down starts with the truth that we are all Human beings with a spiritual core of the Oneness and Equality of All, which holds out our Holistic framework that advances and expands us all consciously and transparently through the Whole. The Buddhists say the openness and warmth of *bodhichitta*—our enlightened mind—is our true nature and condition. Through the body-mind-spirit continuum the Holistic framework "frames" our Higher minds into our Natural Reality of Life, Liberty and Happiness where life is enlightening at the same time that it enlightens, freeing at the same time that it frees, nurturing at the same time that it nurtures, perfecting at the same time that it perfects—all translating into openness and warmth of the Human Race as our natural disposition.

---

[43] "Misguided U.S. Economic Policies Drive Many Mexicans to Come Here," Manuel Perez-Rocha:
http://www.informationclearinghouse.info/article25965.htm

The framework itself fulfills the teachings and tenets of all Religions through time while at the same time capturing a visionary way in which we are experiencing the Earth. The vision expands and advances us into the euphoria of Love itself, and from there on we have shed the old world of ignorance and darkness to shine the Light from a new place and a new space on all that is God (and good) again.

The ethical framework is *free of all politics* as it is the Truth that sets us free from a Fear-based, divisive and violent world and leads us to one where Love is the experience and whose time has come for an upside down and back-to-front highly diminished world.

Based in the reality of Truth—Love, Light, Life itself and the Family of Universal Man—the ethical framework enables us to pick up the drive of the American Revolution of 1776, and carry it through to "the Union" of the Civil War—a (sublime) Union "older than the Constitution" itself Abraham Lincoln said in 1861, and now, in our matured world and wisdom, *complete the American experiment* through being able to "govern ourselves without a master" as Thomas Jefferson fearlessly said that we could.

And so we do, making the *other choice for Humankind* to travel the spiritual path of Peace and Plenty *for all* as the Hopi Prophecy has foretold now without the evil of manufactured war.

Life, Liberty and Happiness as the unalienable rights we find in the American Declaration of Independence are living the fullness of life as one Humanity through the unity, prosperity, happiness and comfort of the Human Race through the fulfillment of all its needs—and through the way we are designed naturally—whole, compassionate, giving, joyous, free, creative and self-autonomous in all the colors and expressions that we are, leading ourselves to new frontiers of Soul.

Laying it Down through The Spiritual UN—Our Leading and Self-Guiding Principles for Our Self-Autonomy

In our consciousness of Love, a new dawn makes a new day and way that is good to all. "Governing ourselves without a master" means to be masters of our own lives with principles that simply open and show the way, where there is no need for rules because everything is just right—in balance with all and in joy with all. Only through the principles of the new way can we be truly free and in peace so that we can ascend to the greater levels of potentiality within ourselves and life to light up the world in our own highly individualistic ways *together*.

Our **Leading Principles** frame the Ethical-Holistic Framework of our true and Natural Reality of our new world and are seen here in letters A–E:

- A. The Department of Spiritual Evolution and the Expansion of Consciousness through the Good, True, Beautiful and Right

B. The People's Usury-Free Money for the Good Stewardship of the Economy
C. The People's Care of the Home Planet
D. The People's Well Being
E. The People's Forward Momentum

Our **Self-Guiding Principles** follow in their numbers and simply unfold the Leading Principles as we see here:

A. The Department of Spiritual Evolution and the Expansion of Consciousness through the Good, True, Beautiful and Right

1. The Department of the Oneness of Life—Liberty and Happiness (Freedom with Responsibility)

All else flows and fills out the Ethical-Holistic Framework through the following Leading Principles:

B. The People's Usury-Free Money for the Good Stewardship of the Economy[44]

1. The Department of The People's Creative Oil Serving God Not Mammon[45]

---

[44] For an exposition of these Self-Guiding Principles (2 to 5), see Chapter 9.

[45] Next to usury-free money for the good stewardship of the economy as the Leading Economic Spiritual Principle is Creative Oil as the second key economic spiritual principle of serving God not Mammon, where money works for Man in the equality, respect, evolutionary progress and service of all Life—see Chapters 5, 6 and 7—and not the other way around where Man is simply living to work for money and is constantly in the survival mode in the usury-war-debt-taxes system, and by extension, Monolithic-Monopoly Business that is destroying all—see Chapters 6 and 9.

2. The Department of The People's Social Credit[46]

3. The Department of Sovereign Manufacturing and Trade

4. The Department of Equity Banking at Set Profits

5. The Department of Zakāt (in Lieu of the Income Tax)

C. **The People's Care of the Home Planet**
   1. The Department of Air, Sky, Atmosphere and Ionosphere

   2. The Department of the Environment, Natural Laws and Healthy Ecosystems

   3. The Department of Animal Well-Being, Respect, Rescue, Preservation of Family Units and Migratory Animals

   4. The Department of Clean, Non-Harmful, Universal Free Energy

   5. The Department of Holistic Science, Technology and Research

   6. The Department of Fish and Marine Life Recovery and Preservation

---

[46] For a viable economy and the happiness and prosperity of *all* people, Social Credit helps keep all the money we need circulating in the economy. See Chapter 9 and further:
http://www.thespiritualun.org/socialcredit.htm

7. The Department of Organic and Biodynamic Agriculture

8. The Department of Clean and Non-Toxic Seas and Oceans

9. The Department of Sound and Cetacean

10. The Department of Minerals and Earth Energy

11. The Department of Non-Toxic Manufacturing and Industry

D. **The People's Well Being**
   1. The Department of Business, Trade, Human Rights and Freedom[47]

   2. The Department of the Positive Success and Prosperity of Small Businesses and Farms

   3. The Department of Safe, Non-Toxic, Harmonic Transportation

   4. The Department of Holistic and Preventative Medicine

   5. The Department of Revitalized Food and Alkalinity

   6. The Department of Progressive Welfare Housing

   7. The Department of Healing Prisons

---

[47] All interlocking concepts. However, bad corporations are the toxic extension of a bad economic system. See Chapter 9.

8. The Department of Mind-Enhancing and Earth-Enhancing Architecture

9. The Department of the Fulfillment of Fundamental Human Needs

E. **The People's Forward Momentum**
   1. The Department of Cosmic Man Education[48]
   2. The Department of Perennial Philosophy and Meditation
   3. The Department of the Comprehension and Development of Manners, Morals and Character for the Building, Uplifting and Forward Progress of Man
   4. The Department of High Art and Culture
   5. The Department of Cosmic Calendar and Rhythmic Cycles
   6. The Department of Magnetic Earth Grid, Song and Cetacean
   7. The Department of Animal, Plant and Mineral Telepathic and Sensory Communication and Weather Balance

---

[48] "Man" is pertinent to both men and women. The term "man" comes from the Sanskrit, *manas*, which means "mind." The Human Race originates from the One Creator *Mind*, and wo-man is representative of the womb of that Infinite Mind.

8. The Department of Heart Centered Communications and Remedial Media[49]

9. The Department of Crop Circles and Space Brotherhood in the Federation of the Peaceful Planets[50]

---

[49] Media with a higher purpose: Remedying all parts of life and the world through the holistic-virtuous realm of the Good, True, Beautiful and Right.

[50] On the Earth planet, we are given fantastic signs and cosmic possibilities in the continuum of infinite life with the relationship itself with higher worlds dependent on Humanity's state of Equality on the Planet—where Equality needs no wars, see Chapters 4 and 7. At the same time, for the unaware and/or the unreflective mind, we mustn't be so self-important or self-centered that we can't imagine life beyond our own nose where higher, more spiritually and technologically advanced life than our own, in harmony with the energetic Oneness of God and Life in the Universe, exists.

In our fraternity with (spiritually-advanced beings of) higher worlds, see the "out of this world" connection of crop circles through their beauty, power, symmetry, complexity and, most of all, creation by highly advanced technology that is in accord with the universal, "no harm" ethic of the Universe—all giving the phenomenon a universal footprint and signature: http://www.swirlednews.com/crop.asp and http://www.cropcircles.net

9 Addendum to Love's Turn on the Planet—An Economic System That Serves Humanity

My fellow citizens of the world, ask not what America will do for you, but what together we can do for the freedom of man.
— John F. Kennedy

"*T*HE RICH WILL STRIVE TO ESTABLISH *their dominion and enslave the rest. They always did . . . they always will. They will have the same effect here as elsewhere, if we do not, by the power of government, keep them in their proper spheres*" wrote Governor Morris, head of the committee that wrote the final draft of the U.S. Constitution.

The power of government to keep what is essentially the Money power in their proper spheres was a prime concern of the American Founders. The Revolution brought about in 1776 was because of this same problem with the Money power as we see in Chapter 4, and later, when the Revolution had been won, a nation is established with great and noble Founding principles as we see in both Chapters 3 and 4—for the prime reason of establishing "God" over the power of "Mammon" which (constantly) seeks to enslave

Humanity in its myriad ways (where outright deception is not out of the equation). It is for this reason Thomas Jefferson gave us the Founding Fatherly advice:

> *"Each generation has a right to choose for itself the form of government it believes most promotive for its own happiness"*—

saying to us that we are not bound by institutional strictures (or structures for that matter) if we see that our collective Happiness can be expressed through another way—which is of course the purpose of this Manifesto as stated in Chapter 1.

Further, less than a century later, Abraham Lincoln in his First Inaugural Address on March 4, 1861—at the advent of the Civil War—had said:

> *"This country, with its institutions, belongs to the people who inhabit it. Whenever they shall grow weary of the existing government, they can exercise their constitutional right of amending it, or their revolutionary right to dismember or overthrow it."*

Through the First Inaugural Address in its entirety[51] we see a definite stand on the Founding Principles, i.e., "the Union"—which is perpetual (universal) and unbreakable (hence the Civil War). The Union, Abraham

---

[51] See: http://www.bartleby.com/124/pres31.html, 12–17

Lincoln said, was formed by the confirmation of history itself through the Articles of Association (1774), and in time, historically matured with the Declaration of Independence (1776) through to further maturation with the engagement and faith of the Thirteen States in the Articles of Confederation (1778) and, to perfect it even more, the Constitution was ordained and established (1787) "in order to form a more perfect union." Nothing can terminate the Union because it is much older than the Constitution and therefore exists forever for Mankind to express in the best way that promotes its Happiness. What can also be noted is that given the same fundamental principles of the American Founding, the conquests of Islam were also the same as the American Civil War—to preserve, uphold and express the unity or *Union* of Mankind (through a unity in diversity) in the effort or jihad to repel tyranny and oppression that had fallen on peoples (including of all prior Religions) worldwide.

Without the God-inspired Founding of America:

> *"We hold these truths to be self-evident, that all men are created equal, that they are endowed by their Creator with certain unalienable Rights, that among these are Life, Liberty, and the pursuit of Happiness"*

and Islam:

> *"In the eyes of my Lord, all people are equal"*—

there would simply be in its place—*when we think about it*—tyranny, oppression and injustice by one group trying to assert its power and oppression over the other.

Further, the above two statements indicate to us that we are to ultimately refer to the morality of God and of his Prophets when political realities are not reflecting the stated objectives through the Founding or fundamental principles as they have been given. God is therefore superior to government, *any* government. Our only duty is to align back with God when there is oppression and violations as a set pattern of a political reality, which we must enumerate as the Declaration of Independence says we should as the cause for the separation from government—so that we may begin again.

Equality, truth, justice (social and economic) are all concepts aligned with God and therefore is the overarching authority over *any* government. Martin Luther King Jr at the same time brought the significance of Justice as integral to the overarching reality which cannot be ignored by any one nation or Humanity anywhere:

> *"Injustice anywhere is a threat to justice everywhere. We are caught in an inescapable network of mutuality, tied in a single garment of destiny. Whatever affects one directly, affects all indirectly."*

The American Founders brought into our view through the Declaration of Independence that there is not simply one, but two existing, *separate* over-arching realities possible

An Economic System That Serves Humanity

for Mankind—that being God or Mammon—where the former offers "perfection," and the other offers "corruption." Abraham Lincoln further acknowledged the existence of the two over-arching realities by clarifying the corrupting one which inevitably and ultimately brings us to the point of weariness—because our institutions are over-taken or have been co-opted by the forces of oppression—at which point there is the Constitutional right of the people to amend the government, and if that no longer works, there is the Revolutionary right to dismember or overthrow it.

The concept of Peace itself is the holding down (literally) of corruption. When Gandhi was asked, "Can people be made to be good?" he answered, "No, all that's possible is to create conditions in which it will be easier to choose good." Peace is not simply then an inner condition ("greater jihad"—see Chapter 3, page 20), but must also be accompanied by an outer condition, i.e., the holding down of corruption so that God, or "the good" Reality, may be expressed—i.e., all that which emanates from our higher or Divine nature as the Good, True, Beautiful and Right where each is the other and is ultimately moral thought that is to essentially perfect (and evolve) us Humans—all of us.

The outer condition is the System, which is to condition us to our perfection:

> *When there is a good system, even evil men cannot do evil, but when there is no good system, even good men may not do good, they may be forced to do evil.*
> — Deng Xiaoping

God is the Reality that conditions us for the expression of perfection, and Mammon or the Money power is the corrupting force—both possible through the outer condition or the System, and either of them *cannot exist with the other:* "You cannot serve both God and Mammon" (Matthew 6:24)—for both offer completely different worlds or realities. The System is the Government—irrespective of party—for the overarching principle is—is it God or is it Mammon?

God engenders "Life, Liberty and Happiness" and Mammon is the reality of the opposite. Are we experiencing more of life, liberty and happiness or less of it? Time is telling us, as we see in Chapter 1, that we are experiencing less of it. Therefore, it is time to make the choice to travel the right path as a collective: the violent and violate path of war and technological destruction, or the spiritual path of peace and plenty for all as the Promised Life of the Creator.

The right path is obvious to The Spiritual UN which has made the latter choice, converging with the desires of the American Revolution and a return to the Union as laid down by Abraham Lincoln—perpetual, universal and unbreakable.

However, "Perpetual War" and "Terror" as our world reality break the expression of our perpetual Union as a Humanity—we are living in Error—therefore it is necessary to lay down the Holistic World Planetary Paradigm of our Wholeness and Oneness to again pick up our desire for a "more perfect union" to now put Mammon in its proper sphere, (literally) holding down all corruption that we may "create the conditions where it will be easier to choose the good" (Gandhi), or the good system where "evil men cannot do evil" (Xiaoping).

Our maturing through time has revealed to us that we must now make the economic solution of usury-free money—the Fifth Fundamental Pivotal Principle in both America and Islam (Chapter 4)—the sound foundation upon which the other Four Fundamental Principles (Chapter 3) can express, flower, evolve and fulfill the Human to perfection in the Reality of God—in place of the corrupting and enslaving force of Mammon as it is leading us to the demise (entropy) of ourselves and the Planet.

At the same time, political parties derive from the same *form* of government—for they have their basis in Mammon, i.e., they exist on an economic foundation that is usurious to begin with—through the "income" tax—that is simply interest paid to the Central Bankers for the printing of the nation's money, on the nation's own printing presses.[52] It is because of this "unsound" foundation to begin with that nothing is ever resolved or solved, people stay divided, Human needs remain

---

[52] See: http://www.thespiritualun.org/federalreserve. Think about this also: Thousands of dollars are (fraudulently) taken simply from one individual each year through income taxes. Multiply that by millions of people in a nation, and you have trillions of dollars each year, i.e., "way, way over the top" money given to the government that simply creates and self-perpetuates more and more corruption—until our whole world and reality becomes that—i.e., one tyrannical and oppressive dark *mess* leading us to entropy.

unfulfilled, problems multiply and wars are fomented. It is why it says to us in the first Chapter of this Manifesto, "Begin Again."

And so we are to "Begin Again"—this time on a *sound economic foundation* to form an *even more* perfect union through a new way of governing ourselves that is synchronized with God,—i.e., the Original Giver of our Rights for the Union in Perpetuity that effects our Happiness. How do we know that? Because the Leading and Self-Guiding Principles in Chapter 8 make it self-explanatory—they create more life and more liberty on the Planet that allow us higher realities through a higher Love that rightfully and responsibly expands our Humanity with all where nothing harms and all helps—making politics and political parties anywhere and everywhere obsolete for the principles themselves are self-governing. We have evolved.

As we sum it up in Chapter 7, the framework for our fundamental Human Needs allows us to lay down the right purpose of money in complete accord with our Humanity and the well being of the Planet at the same time (we are One with all)—as we keep Mammon in its proper sphere. What we take from it all is that money is to serve Man and the well being of the Planet and all living things, and NOT the other way around where Man serves money—Mammon—or is under the control of money, or where money—being the only value of Human and all other life on the Planet—is wrecking, killing, harming, maiming and destroying all.

At a glance, the uplift of all nations resides in "throwing off"—as in the American Declaration of Independence—debt-slave labor "globalization" otherwise known as the "Money power," or in religious, spiritual and moral terms, Mammon.

The sound economic foundation locks in the Founding Principles of America through the Leading and Self-Guiding Principles to "Begin Again"—and to "govern ourselves without a master" as Thomas Jefferson put it—in our new form of government which now sits on the sound six-part interlocking economic foundation of:

1) Debt Repudiation. See the religious basis for debt repudiation in Chapter 4, page 34, and also the (democratic) idea of *"we never agreed to be in your debt"* quoted from "An Open Letter to Wen Jiabo and the Chinese Government," by Kyle Bennett,[53] and from the website, "Odious Debts"—where it says in an article on Argentina that the Federal Court made a landmark ruling that "puts blame [squarely] on the shoulders of corrupt civil servants as well as International Financial Institutions such as the IMF."[54]

2) Nation's Full Sovereign Right to Print and Issue Its Own Interest-Free Money

The nation is to be secured in the full sovereign right and ability to print and issue its own paper money, interest-free, requiring no income taxes for payment, and expressly,

---

[53] See: http://repudiatethedebt.org/2009/09/open-letter-to-wen-jiabo-and-the-chinese-government

[54] See: http://www.odiousdebts.org/odiousdebts/index.cfm?DSP=subcontent&AreaID=152

as we see in the American pre-Revolutionary War experience: "for the purpose of making the goods pass easily from the producers to the consumers" (Benjamin Franklin see Chapter 4).

Further, as the economic system is to serve Humanity, and not the other way around, money's purpose is further defined through the concept of "Creative Oil"—where money is to work for the good stewardship and caring for the Planet and all people as we see in Chapter 7, where everything and everyone is progressing in a compassionate and humane and uplifting manner (with harm to none)—unfolding greater levels of life, liberty and happiness for all on the Planet or in a nation.

In turning the economic system right side up, money is thus working for people, through their own passions and soul purpose (dharma), and no longer is it people working *for* money, or becoming slaves to money, or giving their souls to money, simply to survive.

3) Social Credit—For the end of inflations and deflations, recessions and depressions.[55]

A regular Social Credit dividend check (from fiat money, usury-free) to allow the necessary direct purchasing power of the householder to dictate business needs, which in turn create plentiful jobs—and which in turn creates the learning of even more diverse skills for more Human beings.

---

[55] More on social credit at: http://www.thespiritualun.org/socialcredit.htm

Social Credit is inclusive of the economic spiritual principle of "Creative Oil" of serving God not Mammon (see previous Chapter 8 footnote 45) and is the non-usurious economic system of design to be totally self-contained, self-sufficient and stand alone where it will:

i) *secure the nation's people from predators* that are generated through the imposition of the inflationary and deflationary cycles; Social Credit is fiat money from the people, to the people, and for the people, so the market and profit system serve us instead of interest, monopoly and rent;

ii) *generate prosperity and innovation* through the success of small businesses and farms now that there is sufficient money in the household sector for start-ups and expansions, and at the same time, *profit,* not borrowing is now the financing engine for economic growth;

iii) *end poverty* that the usurious system has imposed on Humanity, with the added benefit of no more destruction to the land and ecosystems—i.e., being in the survival mode where the environment no longer matters because of the dire conditions of Human hunger, starvation, poverty and hopelessness—an example being with the indigenous peoples where their land and way of life that had been previously in harmony with the Earth is now *all* destroyed, including precious sacred sites, through mining, commercial logging and other practices of "development aggression";

iv) *channel science and technology in the right direction* where they are no longer diverted to making missiles, H-bombs, shock and awe and all other Human Race- and Planet-ending technology; instead, Human brain power is now working for—or like—the Fords, the Buckminster Fullers, the Walt Disneys, the Nikola Teslas and the Royal Raymond Rifes[56] where we are creating more and better with less—with the built-in parameter that all is harmless and non-toxic to the Planet and to the health and well being of the body-mind-soul continuum;

v) *align with a futuristic, spiritually-correct reality* where Humans as a Race are no longer working to live, but living to work through their God-given passions and talents—which applies to each and every Human being on the Planet, including the poor and impoverished, for each and every Human being carries the Divine spark of unlimited potential to expand Creation; and, most of all, we are in it together in the most joyous way as life is designed for us by the Original Design of the Creator:

---

[56] Royal Raymond Rife was a scientist in the early 20th century who discovered an electronic treatment that could eliminate every affliction known to man, including cancer. The treatment was painless with no side effects. However, the technology, along with the genius of his work, was suppressed by the pharma-drug cartels of the same usurious economic system inimical to Humanity's interests that we are remedying here. See: *The Cancer Cure That Worked! Fifty Years of Suppression*, Barry Lynes (Mexico, Marcus Books: 1992)

An Economic System That Serves Humanity

This is the sea into which our individual rivers flow where we like dolphins can play and be happy together without war, without usury, without one group always trying to take from the others when man is made for delighting others with what our unique being can create for each other's benefit. Of such is the Kingdom of God.
— Dick Eastman, teacher of the system of Social Credit

Finally, our new-found freedom, of both time and money, goes hand-in-hand with the development of our manners, morals and character so that Human life is nurtured to express the better part of him- or herself and does not get wasted. This can all be a part of our society and culture to build the Man—through which we build The City.

4) Sovereign Manufacturing and Trade—The end of slave labor with worker, environmental and consumer protections as set by the citizens of a nation.

Manufacturing sector must remain within the country through labor and capital and not foreign owned. Foreign exchange must buy goods in same currency as the nation without investing in that nation so as to avoid local currency flight and monopoly buying from recipient nation, i.e., "everything made in China" syndrome.

At the same time, the prevention of capital and currency flight is to overcome the degradation of Human life and the environment. Businesses can import and export through balanced and fair trade as it is to benefit the domestic economy. However, they will not be allowed to produce in foreign countries so all exploitation abroad, as well as locally, can end—i.e., where slave labor, degradation of the environment and consumer poisoning and harm through capital and currency flight have now generated the same realities on both ends.

5) Equity Banking at Set Profits—Depositors lend to banks at 3 percent and banks lend out at 6 percent

No more fiat money, control over the money supply, monopoly credit and predatory lending. Banks remain simply as a business, with 100 percent reserves, in a partnership with its clients with fixed term deposits to keep the money circulating—from borrower to home owner to farmer to entrepreneur—to build people's lives and societies—as the chief operating principle for banks—a principle which can also be deemed Islamic.

6) Zakāt—Using 2½ percent of one's income <u>in lieu</u> of income tax for social services, education and infrastructure as it benefits all. Social services are to include prisons and healthcare, where healing and health in the holistic world paradigm is central to all. See Chapter 6.

Zakāt is the original Islamic edict of the conquests to uplift the poor. It is not only morally right, but is also central to Christianity—all in agreement with the faith and principles of the American Founders and upon which the Revolution was based—see Chapter 4.

In the metaphysical aspect, zakāt, a small percentage of one's wealth—2½ percent—is sourced in God which engenders blessings,[57] whereas the exorbitant income tax,

---

[57] See: http://www.zpub.com/aaa/zakat-def.html

on the other hand, is sourced in debt and usury[58] and is totally unnecessary and wholly corrupt and corrupting as we see in footnote 52 earlier in this chapter. Since usury is one of the biggest sins in Religion and is foisted on all, it would thus lead to collective ruination of the nation and world until this error is rectified.

Monolithic-Monopoly Business is the Toxic and Tyrannical Extension of the Usurious Economic System

Corruption generates more corruption, where the world of Mammon produces destruction in the Natural world,[59] which is God's world—and *not their world* (i.e. Mammon's), to which we are separate and independent of as we are made aware in the opening paragraph of the American Declaration of Independence:

> *"When in the Course of human events it becomes necessary for one people to dissolve the political bands which have connected them with another and to assume among the powers of the earth, the separate and equal station to which the Laws of Nature and*

---

[58] See: http://www.apfn.net/Doc-100_bankruptcy27.htm and http://www.thespiritualun.org/usury.htm

[59] Just as wars are organized violence in the (status quo) institutions of the usurious system, Monolithic-Monopoly Business is the extension of the usurious system through organized and institutionalized greed, destruction, cruelty and poison throughout the Natural world. See Chapter 6, as well as the comprehension of "The Commons of Man" at the end of Chapter 10.

of Nature's God entitle them, a decent respect to the opinions of mankind requires that they should declare the causes which impel them to the separation."

Thus, we find, the tangible causes that impel us to the separation (from Mammon) are the result of Monolithic-Monopoly Business which has artificially replaced and *monopolized* the Earth's (i.e. God's) own Natural order, processes and remedies with its poor imitations and, at the same time, has become the pathological environment, i.e., an *unhealthy womb* through which we must live and consume—chemicals, pharmaceuticals, poisons, toxins, carcinogens, artificial hormones, antibiotics, pesticides, depleted uranium, heavy metals, radiation and genetically modified organisms and foods.

Monolithic-Monopoly Business is also the structure that enslaves, steals and cripples the life force of millions of Human beings including children through child labor. It has made the world this way, not only for profit *and war*, but in order to control and own people from cradle to grave which is all wrong and a crime in itself. In order for the Human species to survive, and as the Declaration of Independence states, a separation must be made from the world of war and weapons, and all that it entails, to the new way of the Planetary Consciousness. That consciousness is the Holistic World Planetary Paradigm of our Wholeness and Oneness. It is a clear contrast and separation from war and militarization of the Error world, returning us, essentially, to all things Go[o]d and Love, as the Laws of Nature and of Nature's God compel us to do.

Robert F. Kennedy said, "Make gentle the life of this world. Let us dedicate ourselves to that." We cannot accept a world that is, in actual fact, annihilating all, and so by making the separation from Monolithic-Monopoly Business, including the "Federal" Reserve which is simply another corporation[60] which has done us all harm, we have, as an intelligent species, the opportunity to begin again.

We, like our Forefathers, have seen that there can be neither democracy, nor life, liberty and happiness of The People through the tyranny of Monolithic-Monopoly Business which exists through criminality, insanity, fraud, destruction and deception as the way to control the reality of the world and monopolize all Human life and its well being. Devoid of all conscience and diabolical in nature, It, through its hydra head of petro, chemical, pharma, agri, mining, weapons and war, endangers the viability of the Planet through its utter recklessness and disregard for all life, as well as creating a constant diseased state and arrested development of Humanity through its poisons, toxins, chemicals and carcinogens which at the same time, destroy,

---

[60] See http://www.thespiritualun.org/federalreserve.htm and http://www.apfn.net/Doc-100_bankruptcy27.htm

kill, pollute, harm and sicken the Earth and people, including the animals.[61]

Moving on to another form of governing ourselves, as our *other choice,* we now have a sound and *beneficial* economic foundation which promotes nothing but our Human happiness. Through that foundation, we have many small businesses and farms (taxed by none), as well as the many inventions of benign technology from all The People that hurt and harm none. A new world *opens us* with the printing of our own money, usury-free—where the creative juices, drive and lives of *all Human beings* are now simultaneously freed to pursue what they love—through their heart's desire—along with the fulfillment of all Human Needs and well being (of everyone, everywhere) in the rightful interests of Humanity, in the good system, where even evil

---

[61] For more of an in-depth look at the ways and processes of Monolithic-Monopoly Business, see: "The Corporation," http://www.thecorporation.com/index.cfm?page_id=312 and Monsanto, the prime example of destructive technology in the natural world (what the Hopi Prophecy foresaw as catastrophic to the future of all): http://www.thepeoplesvoice.org/cgi-bin/blogs/voices.php/2007/03/22/the_silent_war_on_the_people_of_india

We have already seen a slice of Monolithic-Monopoly Business tyranny on the Planet in the suppression of hemp as the natural, *non-toxic* product for a myriad of commercial uses on the Planet in footnote 25, page 57; the suppression of technology that can cure all Human disease, including cancer in footnote no. 56, page 94; the global parameters of a monopoly corporation that require a diseased state (and the consequent arrested development) of Humanity on page 56; and the unnatural, toxic and highly diminished world they have created for us in Chapter 6.

men cannot do evil, on God's free Earth, *at last for all* through the Gentle Path.

And do not think that we cannot again have the world that was already tried and true, prior to America's Revolutionary War:

> *"There was abundance in the Colonies, and peace was reigning on every border. It was difficult, and even impossible, to find a happier and more prosperous nation on all the surface of the globe. Comfort was prevailing in every home. The people, in general, kept the highest moral standards, and education was widely spread."*

The difference now being that we are *simply* One HUMAN Race, anywhere and everywhere on the Planet, and far greater than we know.

10 The God-Forward of Evolution and the Pro-Human Way of Life Through the Holistic World Planetary Paradigm of The Spiritual UN—Wholeness, Oneness and our Union Magnified

> *It is our duty as men and women to proceed as though the limits of our abilities do not exist. We are collaborators in creation.*
> — Pierre Teilhard de Chardin

MUCH HAS BEEN SAID ABOUT Darwin's evolution in our social life, but little about Teilhard de Chardin's conscious evolution in our Planetary life. If we took a bird's eye view into it all we would see two very different worlds: one world is of Fear and animalistic, and the other is of Love and humanistic. The Fear world is of domination and ego, built on selfish gains and violence, while the other is of equality and compassion built on caring and gentleness with all life. The Fear world draws on our worst instincts, while the world of Love draws on our best instincts. The old United Nations is about division and fight, and The Spiritual UN is about unity and peace.[62]

The Spiritual UN is born to understand "Religion," which has been propagandized and politicked to such a point where it has lost its essential meaning. However, we do find Religion's real or true purpose in the Latin origin of the word: "re-ligare," from *re* ("again") and *ligare* ("to bind," "to reconnect" or "to unite"). But what can we say we are binding, reconnecting or uniting *with*? When we study all the Religions and wisdom traditions we find that it is binding, reconnecting and uniting with our true Self, our higher Self, our Source or God. In other words, Religion is about going toward our Source, a going "Home" (toward Light)—our true Home from which we have been separated while in this three-dimensional material world. In that separation we live simply in our ego—hateful and fearful of "the other." Ancient wisdom tells us that the world of materiality and ego is "maya" or an illusion, not our real life. It is not a happy life because it is a destructive life. At the same time, it contracts, instead of expands, or devolves instead of evolves.

Devolution brings us back to the ego, and its world of depression, despair, destruction and suffering, while Evolution brings us back to Source and its world of expansion, joy, bliss and creativity. Imagine the world of simply

---

[62] The Holistic World Planetary Paradigm of The Spiritual UN is naturally *of, by and for* all the people's simultaneous well being, prosperity, progress and conscious evolution: http://www.thespiritualun.org

bliss, joy and creativity as our true world, and what we all wish for ourselves and for each other: peace, joy and goodwill to all men (i.e., all members of the Human Race) is a living reality. That is the path of The Spiritual UN because it is a higher world existing already in all Human hearts.

Religion, Spirituality and Reality: Regaining Our Balance Through the Oneness of Life

At the same time, The Spiritual UN creates the bridge for Religion, Spirituality and Reality so that we, as a Humanity, are able to regain our balance where all are able to live—animals, humans, environment and the life of the ecosystems—through the proper foundation of the Oneness of all Life. No Religion or wisdom tradition is exclusive of the other: all are needed to put together the pieces of the puzzle that enable us to live, to comprehend life, and thus live our highest and fullest potential as Human beings in total joy and creativity with all. The social ethics and morality found in all Religions and wisdom traditions, including the moral philosophy and holistic psychology of the Western tradition, are all a great body of ethical thought that enables us to live a life of meaning, to access and align with higher levels of consciousness and thereby interact with, discover and experience new ways and worlds on our own Planet.

Indeed, the ethics and morality within Religion are our training wheels to (inwardly) "see" better, and thus to know better and, consequently, to live better. At the same time, what we have discovered in quantum physics has already been taught to us in Religion: that life is One. All is One. God is One. There are no separations or divisions or exceptions. What is real or Reality is our Oneness, and overlapping this Oneness like waves on an ocean is our consciousness. Our creative job on the Planet is to simply build on and with the Oneness in a sacred way—respecting all—through our diversity of thought that enables us to discover more of ourselves or more life, which translates to higher levels of consciousness or reality on the Planet. From a bird's eye view we now have our humanistic world far removed from the fear, domination and greed of the animalistic world.

At the same time, spirituality is the bridge between Religion and Science—between the inner and outer worlds. It allows us to enter the world of the immeasurable Unknown whose depths we have not yet imagined. One aspect or dimension of the Unknown is the placebo effect: that miracle of health and healing that occurs simply through the intention of health—and nothing else. In our humanistic world what we need to know is that consciousness, i.e. our world, is our clay and our individual minds through our inner worlds are the instruments to change the condition of the outer world. Everything in Life responds to Love, which is the Source and design of the Universe and at the same time is the underlying sacred Oneness of all Life which translates into the world reality of infinite possibilities and miracles—most pointedly remembered during the times of Christ and his teachings.⁶³ In contrast, Fear, the parameter of the animalistic world of War and militarism (as in standing armies) is not our true world or life—which is why we have the manifestation of conscience to return us to the sacred Oneness of all Life.

Conscience, like an all encompassing sign post, tuning fork and lighthouse, points (back again) to who we are and where we must be. George Washington, the great American Revolutionary and Founding Father, said, "Conscience is a little spark of celestial fire"—it puts us right with (the universal) God and (the underlying light of) our Sacred Oneness. Lose it, and we lose ourselves and our place in life. Separate from it—in any way, shape or form—and we cannot live with ourselves. The consequences or end result—suicide—speaks for itself.

The Spiritual UN is about living with others—in all our colors, cultures, religions, creeds and traditions—guided and tuned to conscience so that we may have more life in ourselves and, as a consequence, on the Planet. In the Spiritual UN we have created Balance that enables us to travel the path of Love where the feminine creations of caring, sharing and wisdom temper and hold in check the masculine drive for unquenchable power and

---

[63] Jesus, well aware of the Oneness of the universal God's omnipresence, omnipotence and omniscience (or, All Present, All Powerful and All Knowing), said, *"Verily, verily, I say unto you, He that believeth on me, the works that I do shall he do also; and greater works than these shall he do; because I go unto my Father* (St. John 14:12)

the mis-use of knowledge that flips all that is rational to the irrational. With Balance, all is in harmony with Life and all prosper everywhere, including the Planet, which will then reflect it all back as our environment through the "eternal Spring"—a concept we are given in Religion to help us gain full comprehension, knowledge and understanding of how we are to live on the Planet and thereby hit our mark both as a spiritual species and for survival of the species where both realities are conjoined.[64]

Human Diversity and Biodiversity Are Conjoined for Human Conscious Evolution

The diversity of the Human Race through its unique cultures, colors, religions and wisdom traditions all reflect a way to interact with Reality—the Oneness of Life—in an interdisciplinary manner that then has the ability to synthesize and form more complex levels of human Being or consciousness. This consciousness would then give way to new worlds on our Earth, or new ways of being that would expand our Human horizons and scope on

---

[64] In the gentle and just peace of a holy, God-enlightened world and Humanity, *"The wolf shall dwell with the lamb, and the leopard shall lie down with the kid, and the calf and the lion and the fatling together, and a little child shall lead them. The cow and the bear shall feed; their young shall lie down together; and the lion shall eat straw like the ox. The sucking child shall play over the hole of the asp, and the weaned child shall put his hand on the adder's den. They shall not hurt or destroy in all my holy mountain; for the earth shall be full of the knowledge of the LORD as the waters cover the sea."* (Isaiah 11:6–9)

how we are all living harmoniously and in absolute joy with each other and all life. In the visionary writings of Pierre Teilhard de Chardin we see we are unified as One (body of the Christ, i.e., our higher, Divine nature), all pulling together in purpose and direction with the same beauty, ease and grace as geese fly in formation—where the whole (formation) is effortlessly uplifting the one and the one (individual) is effortlessly uplifting the whole at the same time in their journey *together*.

Our unity on the Planet is therefore not about homogeneity or sameness, but simply about coming in closer together (as we have been given principally through Religion), yet remaining uniquely distinct peoples on the planet (our diversity) so that we may form more complex levels of being or consciousness—which is not, and never was to be about simply surviving as we have it now. In other words, we need Human diversity to evolve the Planet (and the universe itself) from its present state to its new state of unlimited possibilities. We Humans in all our colors, cultures, religions and wisdom traditions are pivotal to the evolution of the Earth, for which we have been put here, and in a sacred manner:

> *"O mankind! We created you from a single soul, male and female, and made you into nations and tribes, so that you may come to know one another. Truly, the most honored of you in God's sight is the greatest of you in piety. God is All-Knowing, All-Aware."* (Quran Verse 49:13)

What is being said in Islam, and what the Religion purports in the great body of ethical thought, is that Diversity is God-given so that we may know each other through the heart-soul qualities of respect for one another, and those of caring, helping and sharing where there are no divides between individuals through colors, religions, ethnicities, for each and all carry their own unique pieces that are pivotal for a great Work where the sum parts are greater than the Whole.

Indeed, for any Human being alive to his or her own conscience we find:

> "There shall be <u>no compulsion in religion</u> [emphasis added]: *the right way is now distinct from the wrong way. Anyone who denounces the devil and believes in GOD has grasped the strongest bond; one that never breaks. GOD is Hearer, Omniscient.*"
> (Quran Verse 2:256)

What can be noted here is that Religion is a powerful lens within the great body of ethical thought that allows us the backdrop through which to comprehend and remedy our modern-day failings and allows us, as it says, the independence to interpret reality through our own sufficiently developed moral consciousness—where we are able to have "Speculations on the Nature of Evil" within our present day political context.[65]

---

[65] "Speculations on the Nature of Evil," Connie Cook Smith: http://www.thespiritualun.org/references.htm

Thus, through the lens of a higher perspective we find what is key in the Human Family is that, on the social level, Diversity is the spark of God in all its forms—all Religions and peoples are of the One—none are exclusive of the other. There is no dogma or divides (when conscience is intact), simply bridges (in contrast to barriers) between all, knowing and comprehending the way to live and create with the Source of all Life that we know as the Divine. On the physical level, Diversity is the spark of God through all spheres of natural and planetary life—rocks, plants, animals and Humans—which are themselves levels of an ascending consciousness or awareness that culminates in Humans through God or Unity consciousness.[66] The Hindus, one of the most ancient and spiritually progressive cultures on Earth in its time, knew this sacred aspect of Reality. In the Upanishads—the culmination of Vedic thought—we find that all life on the Planet is Awareness at different states of Consciousness, from the dream state to simply awareness, to *self*-awareness and then (with much effort) to human Enlightenment where one sees, as the Holy Rishis (or ancient seers) did then, that "Atman is Brahman"—*soul is God*, i.e., we are all and everything and, at the same time, have all and everything *within*.

"God is everywhere," the Sufis say, and the Christians say "God is Love." Indeed Jesus said to Love God "with

---

[66] Notice also, it is only our Planet Earth, in our solar system, that has this range of diversity, uniqueness and beauty of life that is all sentient—created for us to seek and know God as wisdom texts point to.

all our hearts, might, minds and strength."[67] Moses gave us a foundation to build Love for one another through the Ten Commandments—and absent that foundation we still make War today through coveting, thieving, stealing and killing, along with the rest of the ills of society. The Buddha asked us not to support those who make weapons and poisons. And in every Religion and wisdom tradition, from Jainism to Confucianism, there exists the Golden Rule to "Love our neighbor as ourselves,"[68] which we find from Christ's teachings in the two great Commandments is the same as loving God.[69] We are divinity because Divinity exists in us—there is no separation at the Source.

When we acknowledge life as Divinity we can then see as the Native Americans and other native cultures of the Earth see. Here is what Chief Seattle wrote to the United States government in 1852, in response to its enquiry of buying the tribal lands:

> *"The President in Washington sends word that he wishes to buy our land. But how can you buy or sell the sky? The land? The idea is strange to us. If we*

---

[67] Matthew 22:37

[68] "The Golden Rule," World Scripture: http://www.unification.net/ws/theme015.htm

[69] "'Thou shalt love the Lord thy God with thy whole heart, and with thy whole soul, and with thy whole mind.' This is the greatest and the first commandment. And the second is like it, 'Thou shalt love thy neighbor as thyself.' On these two commandments depend the whole Law and the Prophets." (Matthew 22:35–40)

do not own the freshness of the air and the sparkle of the water, how can you buy them?

"Every part of this earth is sacred to my people. Every shining pine needle, every sandy shore, every mist in the dark woods, every meadow, every humming insect. All are holy in the memory and experience of my people.

"We know the sap which courses through the trees as we know the blood that courses through our veins. We are part of the Earth and it is part of us. The perfumed flowers are our sisters. The bear, the deer, the great eagle, these are our brothers. The rocky crests, the juices in the meadow, the body heat of the pony, and man, all belong to the same family.

"The shining water that moves in the streams and rivers is not just water, but the blood of our ancestors. If we sell you our land, you must remember that it is sacred. Each ghostly reflection in the clear waters of the lakes tells of events and memories in the life of my people. The water's murmur is the voice of my father's father.

"The rivers are our brothers. They quench our thirst. They carry our canoes and feed our children. So you must give to the rivers the kindness you would give any brother.

"If we sell you our land, remember that the air is precious to us, that the air shares its spirit with all the life it supports. The wind that gave our grandfather his first breath also receives his last sigh. The wind also gives our children the spirit of life. So if we sell you our land, you must keep it apart and sacred, as a place where man can go to taste the wind that is sweetened by the meadow flowers.

"Will you teach your children what we have taught our children? That the earth is our mother? What befalls the earth befalls all the sons of the earth.

"This we know: the earth does not belong to man, man belongs to the earth. All things are connected like the blood that unites us all. Man did not weave the web of life, he is merely a strand in it. Whatever he does to the web, he does to himself.

"One thing we know: our god is also your god. The earth is precious to him and to harm the earth is to heap contempt on its Creator.

"Your destiny is a mystery to us. What will happen when the buffalo are all slaughtered? The wild horses tamed? What will happen when the secret corners of the forest are heavy with the scent of many men and the view of the ripe hills is blotted by talking wires? Where will the thicket be? Gone! Where will the eagle be? Gone! And what is it to

say goodbye to the swift pony and the hunt? The end of living and the beginning of survival.

"When the last Red Man has vanished with his wilderness and his memory is only the shadow of a cloud moving across the prairie, will these shores and forests still be here? Will there be any of the spirit of my people left?

"We love this earth as a newborn loves its mother's heartbeat. So, if we sell you our land, love it as we have loved it. Care for it as we have cared for it. Hold in your mind the memory of the land as it is when you receive it. Preserve the land for all children and love it, as God loves us all.

"As we are part of the land, you too are part of the land. This earth is precious to us. It is also precious to you. One thing we know: there is only one God. No man, be he Red Man or White Man, can be apart. We are brothers after all."[70]

The God-Forward of Evolution Is Getting Our Human Species Priority Straight through a Planetary Unity of Heart, Soul and Human Spirituality

Indeed, the Planet is a mothering and nurturing force for all. The Native Americans *already knew this* on a *sacred* level. All aspects of the Planet are alive and aware as *feeling*

---

[70] *The Power Of Myth*, Joseph Campbell with Bill Moyers (Anchor Books, 1990), 42–43

beings—all part of one living conscious, intelligent and caring form ("Mother" Earth) as she maintains balance and life-giving properties for all to survive and thrive—something science has picked up through the Gaia hypothesis.[71] On another level, all in Nature is uniquely contributing to the Whole which *as an effect* of their lives gives life for the good of all. Yes, our Planet Earth and all the animals can do quite well without us, thank you very much.

However, it is only when we turn to the thought of Pierre Teilhard de Chardin do we find out that we Humans actually do have a purpose, or more poignantly, a calling on the Earth. We are here to take Evolution forward. And it is simply by our ability to reflect that can we do that. Where other beings are at different levels of awareness—from dream state (plants) to conscious state (animals), we Humans are at a Self-aware level because of our ability to think and *self*-reflect, i.e., a space and a place to both create thought and look at our thoughts as well as to *receive* thought, i.e. insights, intuitions and inspirations for original thought. Further, there is the Human imperative to break through the wall of preconceived thoughts and world views through the capacity to ask questions (the Socratic dialogue) which enables us to move, grow and ultimately perceive the ultimate Truth—the sacred Oneness of all Life. Because of that, we as a species are able to take Evolution all one giant step further. In the

---

[71] Gaia Hypothesis: http://www.daviddarling.info/encyclopedia/G/Gaiahypoth.html

latter part of the Vedas or in Vedantic thought we find that the ground of thought, i.e., where we can look from *and* create original thought, is God; or the "being" part of the Human *Being*—is God!

We have a concurrence here in the thought of St. Paul: "We live and move and have our being in God."[72] Within this great Being, as we find in Vedanta, there are different levels of Human enlightenment which ranges from Cosmic, to Unity, to God consciousness or *Self*-enlightenment—where the Human being becomes so aware of Being as to be all of Creation within his or her *own* being. At this point the Human being sees (and knows) every part of Creation as an aspect of him- or herself, from the honey bee to the distant star. The only drawback to all this is that we never came knowingly with this awareness. At the same time it takes a moral disposition, which in itself is a Law or door, to open up awareness to Self (or God) and this starts with conscience.

Enter the Prophets of time, or rather, an Awareness in time. Each gave us a body of ethical thought that kept us on track with our conscience (and gave us more of life when we pursued it). Having our being in Oneness or Unity or God is why we feel that killing others is against our conscience. This is why we also find "conscientious objectors"—killing other Human beings is against their conscience, i.e., they *feel* that, meaning, they are *feeling the unity* of Being or God. When we see others hurt and feel

---

[72] Acts 17:28

the same pain, including everything else in Creation from stranded whales, to the felling of forests, to the dynamiting of mountains or the loss of anything in Creation what we're feeling is the ground of Being or Unity of all—or God, which is in us all—and the reason we find here: "What you do unto the least of those, you do unto me."[73]

We are not separate from one another, we are all connected and interconnected in a way that gives us the ability to feel Life, and to move Life to grander heights—that was what Christ's life was all about—to pave and enable the way in the social realm of Humans to connect with one another simply on the **level of spirit** (in contrast to laws) and move beyond the material and divisive trap of life to Unity consciousness, which is a personal encounter or disposition: "I and my Father are One."[74] This same point of consciousness is within all. It is what Teilhard de Chardin termed the "Omega Point," the supreme point of both complexity and consciousness that is drawing us all to it as One, and which we can say is acknowledged every time a Muslim in prayer (five times a day) raises his or her index finger up when bearing witness to "The One."

Our purpose on Earth as Divine sparks of Self-reflective ability is to impart the Oneness and Wholeness of Life through the lens of the uniqueness of our own individual beings—all six billion of us—through all our spheres of Human civilization and the whole of Nature.

---

[73] Matthew 25:40
[74] John 10:30

Our Diversity of thought that comes through all the Religions and wisdom traditions and philosophies beginning thousands of years ago, contains a vast body of ethical thought and food for thought that lends itself to immense synthesis, thinking and creativity with the Earth, and as Teilhard de Chardin would say: "united with it in the processes of complexity" that would lead the way to the Omega Point—*"the God-forward of evolution."* It would allow us to be more of essence (substance of God) than ego (selfish desires), which—left on its own—without essence, creates out of Creation.

Take for example, the fact that we would not have "created" the atom bomb that destroys all life on Earth if we stayed in the great body of ethical thought. Within that thought is the heart and soul that unifies us all—with the Earth. The Earth was made for us, just as we were made for the Earth, and to such a wondrous and complex depth of consciousness that Teilhard de Chardin said it was "made round so that friendship may encircle it."

Being for Ourselves—in the True Sense of Helping Ourselves

The God forward of evolution is the convergence of Human cultures, religions and wisdom traditions as the great human Diversity in unity which makes it *pro-human*, i.e., it is for itself, it is for Humanity. "You cannot serve God and Mammon" is what we find in the great body of ethical thought.[75] That body of thought creates balance

---

[75] Matthew 6:24

that in turn would keep the Earth in balance that would then, through our part on the Planet, create the right structures that would not destroy life but would enhance life.[76] At the same time, the right structures, by keeping the Earth in balance, keep ourselves in balance, and while we are doing that, we learn how to treat the Earth and cultivate ourselves to be better Human beings—"care of the soul" is what Socrates said. That caring includes the reality checks of "lust, gluttony, greed, sloth, wrath, envy and pride"—the seven deadly sins we are warned about in the great body of ethical thought—as they trap us within a lower energy or frequency where we would not be able to hear the sweeter songs, sounds and scents of a greater Reality and thus be able to move toward it.[77]

"Sin" simply means "error." What we find then is that the great body of ethical thought *is wisdom*, so that we don't have to—through our lives and life style—live through the pain of life's mistakes—often fatal—that would be made otherwise. The great body of ethical thought enables us to take off the blinders of ignorance and arrogance and grow and evolve together as one Family of *Universal* Man until we discover the vast riches and potential within our own Being—a world in itself that has no need to destroy the Earth's resources and each other in order for it to be, for the Earth is also a beloved part of itself. The great body of

---

[76] See the Five Universal Mandates in Chapter 6 and the structure for our Leading and Self-Guiding Principles on the Planet in Chapter 8.

[77] The Seven Deadly Sins, also known as the Capital Vices or Cardinal Sins: http://en.wikipedia.org/wiki/Seven_deadly_sins

ethical thought was given not to take away our freedom, but to enhance and perpetuate our freedom through the moral realities of transparency, responsibility, accountability, justice and equality—what the Prophet of Islam brought and taught to Humanity as the basis of all inner and outer life (i.e., the greater and lesser jihads), including democracy: "In the eyes of my Lord, all people are equal."[78] And which is the great opening salvo to the American Declaration of Independence:

> *"We hold these truths to be self-evident, that all men are created equal, that they are endowed by their Creator with certain unalienable Rights, that among these are Life, Liberty and the pursuit of Happiness."*

The God forward of evolution is about equality and closing the gap between the rich and the poor. It is about honoring our Diversity and Biodiversity. It allows us all to breathe free and as full Human beings with a greater purpose. It allows the Earth to be what she is for us: a nurturing, mothering and miracle force where the food is natural, nourishing and exhilarating; where the air is clean, fresh and invigorating; where the water is clear, sparkling and healing; and what may have gone unnoticed: the natural laws of physics to enhance and make

---

[78] *The World's Religions: Our Great Wisdom Traditions*, Huston Smith (New York: HarperCollins, 1991), 227

ever more joyful, enlightening and miraculous our life here together on this beautiful blue orb—all for free.[79]

Our natural instinct is not to harm one another, but to help one another. Indeed, the Vedas told us that the essence or purpose of a Human being—our "dharma"—is to help not harm. The Buddha told us not to support those who make weapons and poisons and yet, through the imbalance of our Earth or the irrational construct, we send our taxes for this very purpose to simply destroy one another—along with all life, and in that way, the Mammon or ungodly way, we are losing our Planet. Ed McGaa, Eagle Man said, "There is no second Planet." We must be good caretakers of our own Planet and of each other—which is the Golden Rule that we find in all the major Religions.

The God way or God forward of evolution in the sacred Oneness of all Life (Truth) is the Human way: it cares, it shares, it helps. It has conscience and the light of wisdom, ethic and equality equally in all, and because of that we have no need for a leader because we are made self-autonomous by that very same light within us all.

In the God forward of evolution, diversity of thought is our Natural nature and the effect is spontaneity of our thoughts and choices that do no harm as they originate

---

[79] An example of such energy that does not take from and destroy the integrity—and beauty—of the Earth is unlimited clean energy from the vacuum: Tom Beardon: http://www.cheniere.org http://www.cheniere.org and also, *Breakthrough Power: How Quantum-leap New Energy Inventions Can Transform Our World*, co-authored by Jeane Manning and Joel Garbon: http://www.breakthroughpower.net

through an ethic or a greater Unity that evolves one and all at the same time. Welcome to the world of our spiritual selves where we and every part of Nature are no longer cogs in a machine but neurons or an awareness in the great Divine Mind of Life where its Diversity, by way of its Complexity, draws us to greater Unity or consciousness within God—where Love is the spirit or glue between the atoms that holds our Universe together and Life is what expands it.

Structuring and Transitioning Planetary Consciousness for Life and the God Forward of Evolution

Life is about developing less of the material and more of the tangential—what Teilhard de Chardin said was the inner Divine spark that is significant in Humans. With tangential energy comes consciousness and a corresponding complexity. With increased complexity comes increased consciousness and the force of Evolution itself within us all. The life in the God forward of evolution is about developing consciousness and its corresponding complexity with the whole planet, *simply on the Human level*, structured to support all and advance all with, and including, Gaia (i.e., earth sentience) through our own Creative Oil[80]—in contrast to us supporting and being limited and destroyed by the *error world* and artifice of greed, corporatism, war, militarism and materialism.

---

[80] See Chapters 7 and 8 as we unleash our spiritually inspired love, connectedness and enlightened knowledge as One *intelligent* Race in practical terms

The God Forward of Evolution is our true world that has no enemies, for it exists on the simple, world changing paradigm of "loving our neighbor as ourselves" with the purpose of flourishing, flowering and unfolding the full potential of all life on the Planet. It sees all life as equal and individual and where Human life itself is returned to its rightful station in life of full autonomous existence, i.e., being able to govern our own lives in the full vigor and potential that it has.

In contrast, we are not to live through heteronomy—a concept we find in Kantian moral philosophy where we Humans are simply pushed and pulled around by forces outside of ourselves where our lives and futures are not in our control through constant havoc, hate, fear, contrived confusion and disaster.

In our social realm, heteronomy is the economy that both runs on and is built on the ruin of all, at all levels of life, through the manufacturing of toxins, diseases, death, disasters and wars in a continual chaos and destruction of both Humans and the Planet.

Drawing from the great body of ethical thought will allow us to retrieve more of our tangential energy to "see" more or "see right" as Abraham Lincoln—in his "Second Inaugural Address"[81]—spoke about as a maturing possibility

---

[81] *"Four years ago, all thoughts were anxiously directed to an impending civil war, all dreaded it—all sought to avert it. Both parties deprecated war; but one of them would make war rather than let the nation survive; and the other would accept war rather than let the nation perish. And the war came. With malice toward none; with charity for all; with firmness in the right, as God*

for all nations of peoples and thereby expand consciousness through a Holistic and healing level to greater levels of awareness and Life, as we move, in the God forward of evolution, to our first innovative level of consciousness as *cosmic beings*:

> *"The prime characteristic of cosmic consciousness is a consciousness of the cosmos, that is, of the life and order of the universe. Along with the consciousness of the cosmos there occurs an intellectual enlightenment which alone would place the individual on a new plane of existence—would make him almost a member of a new species. To this is added a state of moral exaltation, an indescribable feeling of elevation, elation, and joyousness, and a quickening of the moral sense, which is fully as striking, and more important than is the enhanced intellectual power. With these come what may be called a sense of immortality, a consciousness of eternal life, not a conviction that he shall have this, but the consciousness that he has it already."*[82]

The God forward of evolution is what we as a species are meant to be on because it is the natural track for this

---

gives us to see the right, let us strive on, to finish the work we are in; to bind up the nation's wounds; to care for him who shall have borne the battle, and for his widow and his orphan—to do all which may achieve and cherish a just and lasting peace, among ourselves, and with all nations." March 4, 1865

[82] Quoted in John Hick's *Classical and Contemporary Readings in the Philosophy of Religion*, New Jersey: Prentice Hall, 1990, 178

Planet. It engages straight with our hearts, giving a whole new world and peace where there truly is a swords-to-ploughshares reality that benefits and uplifts all. With our human Diversity and Biodiversity, the Planet evolves to even greater levels of being and consciousness of amazement and wonder. So it is in the God forward of evolution we return to the Evolutionary track that is set by certain parameters that we find in Teilhard de Chardin's visionary writing. By imprinting ourselves back on the Evolutionary blueprint we will be able to create the tectonic shift of unity needed to re-*move* ourselves as a species from all danger that we are heaping and experiencing on the Planet through our own harm.

By engaging straight from the heart, we are connecting with all members of the Human Race in the spirit of friendship and unity on the people level of the Planet, surpassing the nonsensical bureaucratic level, so that we may lay the concrete foundations, literally, for the right structure with the right intent. That intention on the collective level would be our *one desire for the world we all want* on this beautiful orb: peace, justice, prosperity, goodwill and joy for all. At the same time, that intention is an imperative for these times as Teilhard de Chardin says, like in the Hopi Prophecy[83]:

> ***"We have reached a crossroads in human evolution where the only road which leads forward is***

---

[83] See Chapter 1

towards a common passion . . . To continue to place our hopes in a social order achieved by external violence would simply amount to our giving up all hope of carrying the Spirit of the Earth to its limits."

In the immutable core of the God forward of evolution—the sacred Oneness of all Life which is our only true, Natural and acceptable reality—we have the principles:

1) "No evolutionary future awaits anyone except in association with everyone else."[84]

2) We must bring our tangential energy to the fore. Tangential energy is the Divine force within every Human that leads Evolution, which is dependent upon:

3) The Two Laws of Evolution: (i) the "Law of Complexity Consciousness," which states that a growth in complexity is always accompanied by a corresponding growth in consciousness. However, the Law of Complexity Consciousness is dependent upon (ii) the "Law of Recurrence," which states that nothing can progress until it unifies. These two laws are the blueprint of Evolution.

4) Tangential energy has to be mirrored through the ethic of Oneness and Wholeness or on Unity for it to manifest and express itself.

---

[84] Evolution: http://en.wikipedia.org/wiki/Pierre_Teilhard_de_Chardin

5) Diversity must build Unity.

Returning the Light to America is to rebuild on the imprint on her Great Seal: *e pluribus unum*—"out of many, One"—One Law, One Love, One Peace, One Common Purpose, One Destiny, One Desire, One Human Family, Oneness, Wholeness, One **Unity in Diversity**—our Union perfect and perfecting.

Imprinting on the Great Double Sided Seal of the United States of America is **The Spiritual UN.** It is for the building of the Great Human Common Unity as the greatest of all—our Human Union in the Brotherhood of All. It is a planetary Human initiative and imperative to heal all wounds, to strengthen the tie of Peace with Brotherhood and, at the same time, laying out a total non-violent, non-militaristic pathway for the Freedom and uplift of all of Humanity, which includes the Protection and Care of the Commons of Man that belong to no one, nor one nation, but equally to all through our sharing and caring. The Commons of Man is the whole natural world of the Planet—the skies, the air, the oceans, the seas, the waters, the wetlands, the forests, the mountains, the valleys, the landscapes, the deserts, the soils, the oils, the minerals, the eco systems and all the animals where all are interconnected as one miraculous and breathtaking *harmonic* organism through which we share our life and are able to live our life.

Indeed, the care and protection of the Commons of Man is pivotal to both our survival and existence on the Earth that hinges on our Human Race choice of re-arranging our *national* paradigm—where the "effort" is no longer to Wars, but simply to the health that restores our Humanity and the naturalness of the Earth. In his book, *The Savage Mind* (Chicago: Chicago UP, 1966), Claude Levi-Strauss quotes a native thinker as remarking that *"All sacred things must have their place."* This means things, such as natural resources, aren't optional to the Earth's own processes, but by their very place or existence (this case under the Earth) are *a priori*. That is, by "Being in their place," says Strauss, "is what makes [objects] sacred; for if they were taken out of their place, even in thought, the entire order of the universe would be destroyed."

Chief Seattle clarified the sacred, natural ordered relationship of the Earth with Humans where *"All things are bound together. All things connect. Man did no weave the web of life, he is merely a strand in it. Whatever he does to the web, he does to himself."* We need only look to what the Australian aboriginals have said about uranium mining: *"When holy metals are dug out of Mt. Isa, the end is near"*—to know that what has been said by the indigenous people of the Earth is true: We are destroying ourselves and all life on the Planet, with war-making, militarism and Monolithic-Monopoly Business all being central to it all.[85]

---

[85] See: "Populations Exposed to Environmental Uranium," Leuren Moret: http://www.namastepublishing.co.uk/Populations Exposed to Enviromental Uranium.htm and http://www.thespiritualun.org/lifeordeath.htm. See also, the uncommon sense of Monolithic-Monopoly Business in Chapters 6 and 9

Let us no longer make the end near, by traveling the wrong road, but, now, at the crossroads of our two possibilities, begin again in a new way where the old world paradigm of war-making, militarism and monolithic business has had its day. Instead, making the *other choice* to *join together* for the Planetary Consciousness of the caring of the Whole, we are lifted into the right reality of our shared Humanity, the best of our individuality and a deep appreciation and caring of the Earth—where there is both Peace and Plenty for all.

Through The Spiritual UN, a wave is being made for Humankind to put down our weapons and "Love one another" in the God forward of evolution—simply the pro-Human way to live the good life on Planet Earth: "as above, so below"[86]—laying down heaven on Earth.

~~ ❋ ❋ ❋ ~~

The Union Perfected

There is no fear in love; but perfect love casteth out fear . . .
— 1 John 4:18

---

[86] Hermes Trismegistus, the mystical "unseen" (spiritual-invisible) brought down to the seen (physical-visible world) as *"We look not at things which are seen, but at the things which are not seen; for the things which are seen are temporal, but the things which are not seen are eternal."* — II Corinthians 4:18

The Spiritual UN Conceptual Index

We have it in our power to begin the world over again.
— Thomas Paine

Chapter 1

American Declaration of Independence, God-given rights and the equality of all people everywhere <u>also</u> the purpose of a nation being "under God," 1

American Experiment, perfect conclusion to, through The Spiritual UN, 3

American Experiment, The Spiritual UN completion of the, 5

Beauty, Truth, Justice, Wisdom, the indivisible Whole of, 6
Begin again, Humanity's power to, 3

Choice to end War, on people and Earth, 6
Culture of materialism and modernism, disconnection from the knowledge of the Oneness of All Life and from each other, 4–5

Error Reality, War and Terror, the necessity to turn back to Source of Natural Reality, 2–3

Evolutionary consciousness, Beauty, Truth, Justice, Wisdom and the, 6

Fear paradigm, moving on from, to Love, 5–6

Gentle life, the other choice to Humanity's future, 5
God, corresponds to Natural Reality, a Universal Reality of, Equality, Life, Liberty, Truth, Rights, Happiness, 2–3

Holistic World Planetary Paradigm, The Spiritual UN, and the reconnection to, 3n
Hopi elder, Thomas Banyacya, 4n
Hopi Prophecy, and God's Promise to Humanity, 4
Humanity, choice to end War and disharmony with Earth, 6

John F. Kennedy, mankind and war, 1

Laws of Nature and Nature's God, the basis of Human equality, and separation from tyrannical government, 2
Laws of Nature and Nature's God, Humanity's ally against tyrannical government, 2
Love, and the advancement of all, 5–6

Nationality, an artificial construct by, and for, the world of war, 3
Natural Reality, and the American Founding Documents, universal spiritual principles and ideals, 2
Natural Reality, beginning (world) again, through The Spiritual UN, 3

The Spiritual UN Conceptual Index

Natural Reality, mandate of American Declaration of Independence, 1
Natural Reality, of world, Equality, Life, Liberty, Truth, Rights and Happiness, 1, 2–3

Paradigm, for a new world, 3n
Politics, dissolving ties to, and separating from, 2
Promised Life, engages Oneness and Wholeness, 5

Sacred Circle, Humanity and the spiritual path, 4
Sacred Circle, and the Promised Life of the Creator, 4, 5
Separation, from man-inspired and applied wars and tyranny, 2
Spiritual path, convergence of The Spiritual UN, the re-alignment of the American Experiment and God's Promise to Humanity, 3–4

Technology, driven through arrogance and power, 5
The Spiritual UN, and the Holistic World Planetary Paradigm, 3n
The Spiritual UN, choice of the spiritual path, 3–4
The Spiritual UN, making way for the other choice on the Planet, 5
The Spiritual UN, and the uptake of America's founding purpose, 3
Thomas Banyacya, Hopi message to world, 4n
Thomas Jefferson, and American Experiment, The Spiritual UN, aligning with 3–4
True spirituality, seeks to connect Unity of all life, 1
Two possible pathways, manmade catastrophic earth destruction, or Earth paradise as it was created to be, 5

Two stone tablets, Hopi Prophecy, and the joining together of complementary knowledge, for right existence on Earth, 4 (*also* ancient with modern knowledge)

War, and disharmony with the Earth, Humanity's Error mode in Natural Reality, 6
War, mankind must put end to, John F. Kennedy, 1
War and Terror, corruption of Humanity's Natural Reality, 2
World, re-connection to the oneness and unity of all Life, and The Spiritual UN, 3n
Wrong road, of Humanity, the violent and violate life, 5

Chapter 2
Advancing all, through joy, bliss and fulfillment, 9
Ancient India, enlightened knowledge of, 8–9, 8n
Aristotle, happiness and Human flourishing, how the Human species is to function, 7

Bhagavad Gita, enlightenment of, 8n

Christianity, and the way to God on Earth, 12
Creation, right existence of Humans in, 8–9

Dharma, and advancing all, without harm, 9
Dharma, the importance of, 10 (*also* soul purpose *also* Human purpose *also* right purpose or right existence of Humans)
Dharma, makes all war obsolete, 13
Dharma, moral excellence, the form of a Human, 8–9

Enemies, turning the other cheek to, 12

The Spiritual UN Conceptual Index

Entropy, and the Second Law of Thermodynamics, 10
Equality, organizing principle of all Religions, and the great Ideals, 13
Essence, of Human, fundamental, 8, 9 (*also* dharma)

Fear, and the loss of soul purpose or dharma (*see also* Human purpose), 11

God, and the construct of our world, 13

Human being, form or blueprint of help, not harm, 12
Human beings, natural existence, help not harm, 11
Human beings, not designed for war and killing, 11–12, 11n
Human purpose, all growing Whole with (*also* soul purpose, *also* dharma), 9
Human purpose, designed to save, not hurt or harm, 8
Human Race, war unnatural for, 11

Jesus, and the Two Great Commandments, 12
John F. Kennedy, the effort to end war, 10

Karma, the absence of dharma, 9
Karma, and suffering of the world, 9
Karma, war, entropy and decay, 10
Kevin Carter, and the Sudan famine, 7, 11

Meditation, finding Human purpose, 8 (*also as* individuals, *see* spiritual need, p. 43n, and Whole education, 62–63, 63n)
Military, war, killing, and suicides, 11, 11n

Natural world, goodness of, 9

Perpetual War, error (sin) existence of Humanity, 11

Reflective life, necessity of, Socrates, 10
Religions, and the great Ideals, purpose of, 13
Rishis, of ancient India, 8

Second Law of Thermodynamics, karma and, 10
Socrates, and the unreflective life, 10 (*also* entropy, *also* karma)
Soul, sin and "perpetual war," 11
Sudan famine, and the failure of Humanity, 11
Sudan famine, and Kevin Carter, 7, 11
System of War (also Militarization), John F. Kennedy, 10
System of War (also Militarization), and law of physics that spells world doom, 10

Unity of all life, going against, 11n
Unreflective life, karmic reality of, 10

Vedic period, enlightenment of, 8

War, sin of perpetual, 11, 11n
War and Terror, and entropy of world, 10
World, becoming more than it can be, through our dharma, 9
World, dharma, and the obsoleteness of War, 13
World, and the Human being, expansion of, 9
World, inhuman design of, 10
World, right existence, through the Two Great Commandments, 12
World, right way to exist in, 13
World, suffering of, 9

Chapter 3

Abraham Lincoln, and the higher nature of Man, 19
America and Islam, basis for good things to be made, 21
America and Islam, common moral framework for truth, justice and liberty, 18–21
America and Islam, diversity, progress and the moral context, 22
America and Islam, E Pluribus Unum, One Life under God, 17–18
America and Islam, First Principle of God and Equality, 16–17
America and Islam, Humanity's test, and building of Unity, through Diversity, 22–23
America and Islam, religious freedom and free speech, 18
America and Islam, same blueprint, 16–23
America and Islam, way for unity in diversity, enhancing individuality, 21–22
America, the new Islam, 16
American Founding and national inheritance, sacred purpose for, 16
Animal vs divine nature, and the conclusion of the American Experiment, 19

Bill of Rights, Gettysburg Address, and the pillars of Humanity's Union, 16, 19 (*also* moral documents)

Conscience vs authority, 18
Cultivation of morality and character, the basis of the highest freedom, 19

Entropy, vs dharma and the spiritual path, 15

Equality of all, and the obsoleteness of war, 15
Evil and our animal nature, freeing ourselves from, 21
Evil, turning away all, 20

Freedom vs consumerism, 21

God, Equality and Creation, unfolding of, 15
God, First Principle, all fullness and progress of Human life flows from, 17
God, First Principle, all other principles flow from, 16
God, recognizing through the Equality of all life, 16
God, The First Principle, America and Islam, 15
Government and the individual, framework of and for, mutual goodness, 20–21
Government, moral framework, and the Angels of our better nature, 19

Immanuel Kant, Humanity's necessity for moral uprightness, 21
Islam, conquests and liberty of conscience, 18
Islam, duty to the poor, 18, 18n (*also* zakāt)
Islam, good works are more important than disagreements, 22
Islam, inclusiveness of Christianity, 17–18
Islam, recognition of individuality, 17
Islam, religious inclusiveness, 18
Islam, the necessity of diversity for the building of Humanity's unity, 22

Jihad, greater, inner work of Humanity, 20

The Spiritual UN Conceptual Index

Jihad, lesser, outer work (obligation) of Humanity, 20 (*see also* Militias *also* jihads, greater and lesser, Chapter 10, p. 121)

Militias, The People's back up for the agreement with government, 18–19 (*see also* jihad)
Money, and Humanity's moral existence go hand-in-hand, 23
Moral documents, necessity of, 19
Moral framework, and the enhancement of the individual, 19
Moral framework, the imposition on government, and the prevention of corruption and tyranny, 19
Moral framework, underlies and protects a progressive society, 19

Planet, and the harmless way on, 16
Prophets, purpose of, 20–21

Reason, a weapon for common sense, Thomas Paine, 15
Respect for all, fundamental to America and Islam, 17–18

Second Amendment *see* Militias
Socrates, virtue and knowledge, key relationship, 21
Spiritual path, dharma and true, 15

Ten Commandments, *see* moral documents
Test of Humanity, Islam and America, 22–23
Thomas Jefferson, Humanity, and the purpose of the American Founding, 19, 22
Thomas Paine, reason, a weapon for common sense, 15

Uniformity of thought vs differences of opinion, 17
Unity in Diversity, expression of, 21–22

Virtue, aligns itself with courage, 21
Virtue, character and the enlightened life, Socrates, 21

West and East, and their basis in the First Principle, 15
Whole, all made, 16

Chapter 4
"A more perfect union," manifest of a fundamental morality, 25–26
Abraham, righteous forefather, of Judaism, Christianity and Islam, 36n
America and Islam, Five Fundamental Principles, way for Humanity, full and free existence, 26, 37 (*see also* Chapter 3)
America and Islam, money must be usury-free, 26–32, 33–34
America and Islam, transcendence of nationality, and given to no ethnocentricity, 25
American Revolution, cornerstone and pillar for, The People and money, 32
American Revolution, real cause of, 26, 30, 31
American Revolutionary War, Banker imposed poverty, cause of, 29–32

Benjamin Franklin, original cause of the American Revolution, 30
Benjamin Franklin, and pre-Revolutionary War America, 27, 28, 29

The Spiritual UN Conceptual Index

Blessings, and the "more perfect union" of Humanity, 26

Christianity, Judaism and Islam, *see* Semite Religions
Christianity, the spirit, way and life of Humanity, taking care of one another vs piecemeal charitable contributions, 35–36, 36n
Class differences, Islam and the dissolution of, 35
Congressman Charles G. Binderup, American War for Independence, historical account of, 26–32

Debt and wars, no obligation to, 34

Equality vs War, 37

Five Fundamental Principles, of America and Islam, 26 (*see also* Chapter 3)

God and Earth, sacred relationship between, 35–36, 36n (*see also* Land)
God way, absence of the, 37
Gold and silver money, basis for authoritarian control and tyranny, 29–31

Happiness, God Way vs Tyranny and Catastrophe, 35–36, 36n, 37 (*also* God and Mammon)
Happiness, pre-Revolutionary War America, and the sound and beneficial monetary system of the people, 27, 30–31
Human purpose, and the money system, 32–33

Idealized society, coming together for the upholding of, 36n
Income taxes, basis of usurious money, 26, 31–32

Islam, and the economic, moral and social welfare of the people, 34–35

Islam, and the Evil of usury, 33

Islam, forgiveness of debts and the charitable and ethical heart, of government and people, 34, 35

Islam, nations, and odious debt, 34 (*also* debt repudiation)

Islam, and the observance of the Torah and Gospel, 36, 36n, 37 (*see also* Semite Religions)

Islam, and the progression of the poor, 35, 37 (*see also* Christianity)

Islam, and zakāt, in lieu of the usurious income tax, 35 (*see also* Chapter 9, p. 96)

Israel, original and true meaning of, i.e., not a geographical location or a nationality, but a sacred agreement to uphold God's laws and Prophets, for the idealized society, that effects great happiness for all, 36, 36n (*also* God's Promise)

John Twells, British historian, and the American Colonies, 30–31

Land, belongs to God, for God's Way, 35–36, 36n, 37

Money, a thing-in-itself vs facilitation of Human life, 26, 29–30, 32

More perfect union, morality, and the transcendence of nationality, 25–26

People of God (*also* Light), *see* Abraham

Peter Cooper, and the American Colonies, 31–32

Poverty, absence of, pre-Revolutionary War America, 28

The Spiritual UN Conceptual Index

Poverty, caused by the reduction of the circulating medium of exchange, 30, 31
Poverty, an imposed condition by Central Bankers, 29–32
Poverty, not a concern or sensitivity of the rich (mindset), 27–28
Poverty, right system, and the end of, 37

Quran, and Israel, 36, 36n
Quran, and the observance of Torah and Gospel, 36 (*see also* Semite Religions)

Religions, and the poor, 37
Rich, and the necessity for wars and plagues, inhuman world of, 28
Rothschild central bankers (financiers), and the corrupting influence on governments, 30
Rothschild central bankers (financiers), hiding of their schemes from Humanity, 30

Semite Religions, Judaism, Christianity, Islam, non-separation of teachings, 36, 36n, 37
Serving God, right system, and the obsoleteness of war, 37
System, right, 36n, 37, (*see also* Human purpose)

Taxes and interest, none other than to impose poverty, 31–32
Thomas Jefferson, Man, rights and justice, (no man can be a slave), 25

Usurers, and the theft of Humanity's great potential and purpose, 32–33

Wars, product of the debt-usury system, 34, 36n
Will of God, America and Islam, Five Fundamental Principles, 26 (*see also* Chapter 3)

Year of Jubilee, Man's relationship with Earth, and the moral and spiritual awakening for equality, and equity, 36n

Chapter 5

Agape, level of self-actualization, the third level of collective Human Needs, 41, 44
Albert Einstein, and the proper use of the rational mind vs intuitive mind, 43
Alexander Solzhenitsyn, mankind and its salvation, 39

Balance of weapons, vs balance of the heart, 48
Body-mind-spirit continuum, and the Five Universal Mandates, 46
Body-mind-spirit continuum, fulfillment of Whole Human, 40
Body-mind-spirit continuum, Love and the, 44

Capital punishment, and the Good, True, Beautiful and Right, 42 (*see also* the incarcerated in Chapter 6)
Care of the soul, our spiritual need, and the movement out of entropy, 45
Clean Water, Food, Clothing, Shelter, first level of collective Human Needs, 40–41
Completion, of Human, self-actualization and agape, 44–45
Culture of materialism and modernism, connecting to life beyond, 41

The Spiritual UN Conceptual Index

Design, for evolution and life, matching Creator's perfect, 46
Dharma, and Co-Creators with the universal God, 45
Dharma, self-actualization, and the absence of all karma, 44

Education, and the level beyond, 41
Education, and opening up to the "what" and "why," 41
Education, the second level of collective Human Needs, 41
Entropy, and the unreflective life, 45–46
Equality, enlightens us to our collective Human Needs, 39
Ethic of Wholeness, and our true world purpose, 48, (*see also* Realm of Wholeness)
Existence, the Realm of Wholeness and right, 43
Existence, simply the fulfillment of our Fundamental Human Needs, 40

False reality, of Humans, world of war and weapons, 48
Five Universal Mandates, and the redesign of the Planet, 46, 48 (*see* Chapter 6)
Free movement of people, the Five Universal Mandates, and the re-design of the Planet, 46

Genius, and the deepening of the democratic experience, 47
Genius, self-actualizing ourselves to, 43
Gentle life, and the enlightenment of Humanity, 43n
Gentle life, and the ethic of Wholeness, vs the life out of balance, 47
Gentle life, the fulfillment of our Human Needs, and a return to our God-given Humanity, 40
God, existence of, 45–46

God, and the fulfilling path for all Humans, 40 (*also* dharma, *also* spiritual path *also* God's Promise)
God, our creative relationship with, 45
Good, True Beautiful and Right, the advancement of all, without harm, 43 (*also* Holistic *also* Realm of Wholeness *also* ethic of Wholeness)
Good, True, Beautiful and Right, the indivisible Whole, 42
Good, True, Beautiful and Right, no rules, just right, 46
Good, True, Beautiful and Right, and the Realm of Wholeness, 42–43, 45
Good, True Beautiful and Right, virtue and the, 43

Heartsong, meets Earthsong, and the balance of the heart, 48
Holistic, no rules, just right, through the Good, True, Beautiful and Right, 46, 47 (*also* Realm of Wholeness *also* ethic of Wholeness)
Hopi Prophecy, warning on technology, 39–40
Human Need, to know God, 45 (*also* Source) (*see also* Education, level beyond)
Human Needs, collective, basic, first level of existence, 40–41
Human Needs, collective, second level of existence, 41
Human Needs, collective, third level of existence, 41–46
Human Needs, common agreement in all Religions, the fulfillment of, 39
Humans, true purpose, on Earth, 45

Ideals, transcendent Realm of the Platonic Forms, 42
Ideology, satisfying of Fundamental Human Needs, transcend all, 46
Individual, unique blueprint, on Earth, 44–45

The Spiritual UN Conceptual Index

Individuality, the Five Universal Mandates, and the drive to find our unique, 46
Intuitive mind, vs the rational mind, 43–44, 45–46

Jungian psychology, and the over-preponderance of the rational mind, 45

Knowledge, beyond education of rational mind, 41 (*also* Virtue)
Knowledge and bliss, 43, 43n
Koyaanisqatsi, and life out of balance, 47

Love, fulfillment through the body-mind-spirit continuum, 44
Love, self-actualizing ourselves to, 44

Mankind, salvation of, Alexander Solzhenitsyn, 39
Maslow's hierarchical pyramid of needs, 40
Meditation, facilitates the spiritual need of Humans, 43n
Moral dimension, Life and the, 46–47

"No harm," way of life, on Planet, 44

One Life, religion and science agree, 46–47
Oneness of Life, and the ethic of Wholeness, fits our world, 48

Personal, becomes the universal, brotherly love and the, 44
Pierre Teilhard de Chardin, world and Love, 44 (*also* Human purpose, *also* dharma)
Planet, Holistic, and the ethic of Wholeness, 46–48

Planet, Oneness of Life, and the meeting of Human Needs, 40
Planet, spiritual path and the toxic free, 47
Platonic Forms, the wholeness of Reality, and the Human mind, 42

Rational mind, knowledge beyond, 41 (*see also* intuitive vs the rational mind)
Rational mind, limit of, 41, 43, 44
Rational mind, over-preponderance of, to the irrational, 45
Realm of Wholeness, and the Creator, 45
Realm of Wholeness, exhilarating possibilities through, 45 (*see also* ethic of Wholeness)
Realm of Wholeness, and the Good, True, Beautiful and Right, 42–43
Realm of Wholeness, Holistic basis, no rules, just right, 46–47
Realm of Wholeness, a transcendent ethic and knowledge combined, 42–43 (*also* virtue)
Respect, for all, and the sacred basis of all life, 46–47

Science and religion, Oneness of Life, fundamental agreement, 46–47
Self-Actualization, and the realm of brotherly love, 44
Self-Actualization, and the third level of our collective Human Needs, 41–46
Socrates, the oneness of virtue and knowledge, 43
Socrates, and the unreflective life, 45–46
Spiritual need, and the practice of meditation, 43n
Spiritual need, takes care of Human wholeness, 41–42
Spiritual path, Humanity crossing over to, 47

The Spiritual UN Conceptual Index

Survival mode, and the (perpetual) lack of Human progression, 40
System of war, harmful technology, prophecy and, 39–40 (*also* Militarization)

Technology, Hopi Prophecy, harm vs help, 39–40

Universal way of being, personal is the universal, 44

Virtue, the disposition for the transcendent knowledge, Wholeness and bliss, 42–43
Virtues, vs entropy and addictions, 45

War, Humanity's ability to move on from, 46, 47, 48
Weapons and war, vs our choice for a toxic free Planet, 47
Whole Human, *see* Body-Mind-Spirit continuum
Wholeness, *see* Realm of Wholeness (*also* Self-Actualization, *also* dharma)
Will Campbell, 42, 42n
World, balance of weapons vs balance of the heart, 48
World, growing Whole with Self, 45
World, Oneness of Life, and our true world purpose, 48
World progress, and the fulfillment of our Human needs, true definition of, 39
World, and the spiritual path, end of war and weaponry, 47, 48
World, Humans, God and the static state of, 45–46

Chapter 6
Advancing, Humanity, 50
Agricultural "business" *see* Business

Amazonian Indians, and the tropical rain forests, 52
Animal research, 57
Animals, and God's purpose, 57, 60
Animals, Human morality, and right use of the Earth, 57–60

Body-mind-spirit continuum, education and the, 62 (*see also* Know Thyself)
Business, *also* agricultural "business" *also* pharmaceutical "business" *also* chemical "business" *also* war and weapons "business," 50–51, 56, 57–59, 59n, 60n, 62n
Business vs Health of Planet and Humans *see* Planetary Consciousness vs Monolithic-Monopoly Business

Chemicals, fertilizers, pesticides and toxins, *see* Earth natural
Children, world, education vs war and weapons, 62n
Cruelty, institutionalization of, 57

Dharma, and the fulfillment of our Human and planetary needs, 50
Dharma, and the Planetary Consciousness, 64n
Disasters, and the knowledge gap, 52

Earth, natural, and the elimination of all toxins and chemicals, 52–55
Education, whole, meaning of, 62–63 (*see also* Know Thyself)
Education, for all, and the natural process of population self-regulation, 61, 61n
Eric Encina, and the criterion of a just money system, 49

The Spiritual UN Conceptual Index

Evolution, the wholesome structure, and Planetary enlightenment, 65

Factory farming, 57
Farming, and Mother Nature, 55
Farming, proper relationship with Earth, 52–53
Five Universal Mandates, and the advancement of Man and the Planet, 49–50
Five Universal Mandates, the Oneness of Life, and the Higher Love, 65
Five Universal Mandates, reaching and uplifting every Human being, on the Planet, 65
Five Universal Mandates, and the vote for the pro-Human Way of life on the Planet, vs War and Militarism, 51
Food, Mother Nature, and abundance of, 55, 60

Gandhi, and the moral fiber of a nation, 57
Genetic engineering, elimination of, 55, 60
Geoffrey Anketell Studdert Kennedy, war and the abominable waste, 51, 51n
God way or Mammon way, 50

Happiness, society and the individual, 63
Healing, the world whole, 65
Health vs Business, 56–57 (*see also* Planetary Consciousness vs Monolithic-Monopoly Business)
Health, human and planetary, one of the same, 55
Hemp, wonder plant of Planet, substitute for chemicals, myriad commercial uses, 57n
Herophiles, health and civilization, 55
Holistic medicine vs pharmaceutical drugs, 55–56

Holistic World Planetary Paradigm, dynamic and creative energy of, 64n
Hopi Indians, and mining, 52
Hopi Prophecy, Planet and choice, 57
Human Needs, the Five Universal Mandates, and the fulfillment of, 60–61
Human purpose, on earth, Know Thyself, 62
Human soul, discovering the depth, knowledge and possibilities of, 65
Human species, cogs in a big machine or spiritual beings, 62–63

Incarcerated, Martin Luther King and the, 64
Incarcerated, society and the, 63

Joseph Campbell, 63–64, 63n

Know Thyself, and the Whole education, 62–63, 63n

Land, ethical treatment of, 53
Love, organizing principle of world, vs profit and War, 61–62

Mammon, debt and usury, world of destructive war, weapons and technology, 50
Militarism, collective cancer, feeds on society, to its death, 51
Militarism and war vs pro-Human way of life on the Planet, 51
Monolithic-Monopoly Business, anti-democratic and adversarial to the Planet, 60, 60n

The Spiritual UN Conceptual Index

Monolithic-Monopoly Business, inhumanity, over-consumption, pollution, and the destruction of Human and planetary health, 57–59

Monolithic-Monopoly Business, tyranny of, 57n

Natural solutions and technology, 52

People, free movement of, and the Planetary Consciousness, 64n

Pharmaceutical Drug Business, and the suppression of Human health, 56, 56n

Planet, and the crossroads of our collective future, 51

Planet, non-toxic natural solutions and technology, 52

Planetary Consciousness, dharma, and the free movement of people, 64n

Planetary Consciousness, dynamic and creative energy of, 64n

Planetary Consciousness vs Monolithic-Monopoly Business, 57–60, 64–65 (*see also* Chapter 9)

Planetary Consciousness, and our relationship with God and Nature's God, 60

Planetary Consciousness, prisons, welfare housing and the, 64

Planetary Consciousness, the spiritual path, and the choice of perpetual peace, 65

Planetary Consciousness, upliftment of all, 64

Politics, obsoleteness of, 65

Polluting footprint, and the elimination of Monolithic-Monopoly Business from our Planet, 60

Population, self regulation, and education, 61, 61n

Promise of Creator, and the Five Universal Mandates, Holistic structure, 50

Prophets of God, and the spiritual way, 61–62

Respect, and our whole new world, 60

Self-Actualization, and Love, 63
Self-Actualization, and the meeting of Human Needs for all, 61–65
Serving God vs serving Mammon, choice 50 (*see also* Planetary Consciousness vs Monolithic-Monopoly Business)
Shark finning, 57
Society, and the individual, 63–64
Society, wholesomeness of, 63
Soil, for the health of animals and Humans, the necessity to eliminate all chemicals, fertilizers and pesticides from the Earth, 53–55
Spiritual path, and the end of politics, 65
Spiritual path, and the Holistic structure, 50
Spiritual path, vs Mammon (world built for war, debt, usury), 50

Technology, and inventions, in harmony with all the planetary systems, 52
Toxic reality, war and militarism, 51
Two tablets of knowledge, joining of, and the advancement of all, 50 (*also* ancient and modern knowledge *also* two types of knowledge)
Two types of knowledge, lack of, and disasters, 52

Universal Mandate 1, and the fulfillment of Humanity's First Level of Existence (in the Body-Mind-Soul Continuum), 51–55

The Spiritual UN Conceptual Index

Universal Mandate 2, and the fulfillment of Humanity's First Level of Existence (in the Body-Mind-Soul Continuum), 55–60
Universal Mandates 3, 4, 5, and the fulfillment of Humanity's Second and Third Levels of Existence (in the Body-Mind-Soul Continuum), 61–63
Universal Mandates 4 and 5, and society, 63–65

Vegetarian diet, trend towards, 55, 57–60
Violence, *see* War

War, institutionalized violence, 57
War, perpetual, vs perpetual peace, 65
Welfare housing, society and, 63–64
Whole, healing world, 65
Wholesome structure, Universal Mandates One through Five, 65
Will Rogers, war and civilization, 50
World, built for war, debt and usury, 50–51
World, choice, of organizing principle, profit and War or Love, 61–62
World of weapons, or world of love and enlightenment, 62n

Chapter 7

Albert Einstein, the need for science and religion, and the new consciousness, 71
American Declaration of Independence, and the return to balanced life, 71
American Revolutionary War, cause of, 68, 69
Andrew Gavin Marshall, Humanity, and the imposed state of poverty on Humanity, 67 (*see also* Poverty, in Chapter 4)

Balance, returning to through, American Declaration of
    Independence, 71 (*also* Natural Reality)
Balance, through Nature and God, 71
Begin Again, collective Humanity, from new
    consciousness, 71, 72
Benjamin Franklin, and the pre-Revolutionary War
    experience, 68–69
Blessings, spiritual path, and the Five Universal Mandates,
    70, 70n, 72

Class differences, imposed state of usurious economic
    system, 68
Consciousness, all problems solved from higher, 71, 72
Creative Oil, and the fulfillment of our Human Needs,
    70, 70n
Creative Oil, money as, 69

Dharma, and God, 72

East meets West, Islam and America, and the obsoleteness
    of War, 68
Effort, collective, transferring from War to Peace, and the
    halt of entropy and harm, 67
Equality, needs no war, 68

Five Fundamental Principles, of America and Islam, 68,
    68n (*see also* Chapters 3 and 4)
Five Universal Mandates, 70, 70n, 72 (*see also* Chapter 6)

God, world, and serving, 70–71, 70n
God's Promise, and the Five Universal Mandates, 72

The Spiritual UN Conceptual Index

Good, True, Beautiful and Right, path of, serving God, and fulfillment through, 70–71

Great Commandment, the, re-alignment back to Human soul, 68 (*also* the Two Great Commandments)

Holistic ethic, One Life, the meeting of science and religion, 71

Hopi Prophecy, Humanity, and the two choices, 72n

Humanity's progress together, rift through imposed usurious economic system, 68

Ideal state of Humanity, America's pre-Revolutionary War experience, 68–69

Islam and America, identical fundamental principles, 68, 68n

Lawmakers, obsoleteness of, 71

Love, the origin of Life, Liberty and Happiness, 67

Mammon and God, serving of, 69, 72

Mammon world, usury, debt and war, 70

Money as Creative Oil, and the American pre-Revolutionary War experience, 69

Money as Creative Oil, and the fulfillment of our Fundamental Human Needs, 70, 70n

Money as Creative Oil, the Five Universal Mandates, and the unlocking of our full human genius and creative potential, everywhere, 70, 70n

Money as God over Humans, 69–70

New world paradigm, de-militarized world, and The Spiritual UN, 72

One Life, Humanity and Planet, beginning as, 71

Path of Peace vs War, our collective choice of, 67
Poverty, beggars, unemployment, fraudulent economic system, an imposed state on Humanity, 68
Poverty, and the waste of Humanity, Andrew Gavin Marshall, 67

Respect, creating world of, 70–72

Sacred Circle, and the Five Universal Mandates, manifest through, 72
Serving God, moving from War to Peace, and from doom to bloom, 72
Serving God and Serving Mammon, produces two different worlds, 69–71, 72
Spiritual path, the Five Universal Mandates and God's Promise, 72

The Spiritual UN, chalice for the spiritual path, 72

Usurious bankers, and the imposition of poverty, on Humanity, 69–70
Usurious economic system, and the creation of class differences, ills of society, 68
Usury, America free of, pre-Revolutionary War, 68–69
Usury, dissolution of, and the end of Debt-War system, 68

War, from doom to bloom, 72
War, wrong fit for Human soul, 67–68
Way of life, serving God, 70–71

The Spiritual UN Conceptual Index

World of War, Debt and Usury, imposed, not our true world, 70

Chapter 8

Abraham Lincoln, the union, older than Constitution, 75
America, purpose of, and finishing the work of the Union, 75
American Declaration of Independence, reason for, 76 (a return to Humanity's Natural Reality *see* Chapter 1)
American Experiment, completion of, 75
American Revolution, picking up on, 75
Andrew Gavin Marshall, Human nature, control vs nurture, 73

Balance, and the principles, no rules, just right, 76
Body-mind-spirit continuum, and the Holistic framework of Humanity, 74
Brotherhood of Equality, and the fulfillment of fundamental Human Needs, 73
Brotherhood of Man, grand principles of America and Islam, 73
Bodhichitta, and our enlightened mind, 74
Business, and small businesses, 79, 79n

Caring for The People's Well Being, 77, 79–80
Caring of the Whole Planet, 77, 78–79
Consciousness, Life, Liberty, Happiness, and spiritual evolution of the Planet, 76, 77, 80–81
Crop circles and the Peaceful Planets, 81,
Crop circles, signs and power of benevolent, advanced life, 81n

Diseased state of world, imposed state on Humans and Planet by interlocking usurious system with Monolithic-Monopoly Business, 77n, 79n (*see* Chapters 6 and 9)

Economic spiritual principles, 77n
Economic system, serving Life and Man, no longer Mammon, 77, 77n, 78, 78n
Energy, clean, non-harmful and free, 78 (*see also* Chapter 10, pages 121–122, 122n)
Equality of All, no more disturbance by tyranny, 74
Equality, and the evolution of the world to higher world life and contact, 81, 81n
Ethical framework, picking up on American Revolution, 75 (*see also* Holistic framework)
Ethical-Holistic framework, frames our true and Natural Reality, 76

Family of Universal Man, and the completion of the American Experiment, 75
Farms, 79 (*see also* Chapter 6)
Fear-based world, moving on from, 75

God, Love and Light, 75
Governing ourselves, without a master, and the principles of the new way, 76–81
Governing ourselves, without a master, Thomas Jefferson, 75

Higher worlds, and spiritually advanced beings, 81n
Holistic framework, advancing and expanding all life, 74 (*also* ethical framework)

Holistic framework, fulfills teachings and tenets of all
    Religions, 75
Holistic framework, perfect relationship with individual, 74
Hopi Prophecy, and Humanity's choice, of the other path,
    75
Human beings, functioning correctly to our form, 73
Human Nature, to be nurtured, not controlled, Andrew
    Gavin Marshall, 73
Human Needs, same for all, 73
Human Race, warmth of, natural disposition, 74

Immigration, mass, no need for, 73–74, 74n

Laying down truth, we are all Human beings, 74
Leading and Self Guiding Principles, of Humanity, 76–81
Life, Liberty and Happiness, Holistic framework, frames
    our Higher Minds, 74
Love, and the consciousness of a new day, and the highly
    individualistic way, 76
Love, and the visionary way, time for, 75

Manas, and the origin of the Human Race, 80n
Media, and the Good, True, Beautiful and Right,
    re-instituting proper purpose of, 81n
Media, remedial, 81

New world paradigm, peace and joy of, 73
New world paradigm, world and national problems, coming
    into balance, 73–74
Non-duality of world, and heart-centered communications,
    81

Planet, caring for, in one seamless Whole, 74, 76–81
Politicians, tyrants and bureaucracies, no need for, 74
Politics, no need for, 75
Politics, world free from, 75
Population explosion, failure of fulfillment of fundamental Human Needs, 73 (*see also* Chapter 6, population self-regulation)
Prisons, 79 (*see also* Chapter 6, the incarcerated)
Progressing all, through the Body-Mind-Spirit continuum, naturally, 74

Serving God, not Mammon, 77n
Social Credit, 78, 78n (*see also* economic spiritual principles)
Spiritual path, lifting ourselves out of manufactured war, 75

The Spiritual UN, laying it down, governing ourselves, no need for a leader, 76–81

Union, picking up Humanity's, 75
Usury-war-debt-taxes system, survival mode in the, 77n

War, freeing ourselves from manufactured, 75
World, free from fear and violence, 75
World, and the new frontiers of Soul, 76

Chapter 9
Abraham Lincoln, and the right of the inhabitants of America (the Union), 84
Abraham Lincoln, and the two over-arching realities, of God and Mammon, 87

The Spiritual UN Conceptual Index

Abraham Lincoln, and the Union, 84–85, 88
America and Islam, equality central to, 85
America and Islam, and the sound economic foundation, 89
American Declaration of Independence, and God, 86
American Declaration of Independence, and the separation of Humanity from Mammon, 97–98
American Declaration of Independence, and the two separate, over-arching realities, 86–87
American Revolution, and the clear delineation between God and Mammon, 83

Banks, returning to their proper role, building people's lives and societies, 96
Begin again, the opportunity to, 86, 99
Begin again, why we must, 89–90
Beginning again, without a master, 91 (*see also* Humanity's Leading and Self Guiding Principles)
Building the City, through the Man, 95
Building Humanity's sound foundation, 89

Cancer, and the cure that had been found, 94n
Change, outer world system, the necessary element of, 87–88
Corporations, *see* Monolithic-Monopoly Business
Corruption, and the role of Peace, 87
Corruption, and the system, 87–88
Corruption, income taxes basis of, 89–90, 89n
Corruption, zakāt vs income tax, 96–97
Creator, returning to the original design of, 94
Cultivating Man's genius, for peace and innovation, vs harm and greed, 94, 94n
Current world reality, and Humanity's demise, 89

Debt repudiation, moral basis of, 91, 91n
De-militarized world, and the "more perfect union," Humanity's other choice, 88
Deng Xiaoping, and the good system, 87, 89
Dharma, the unleashing of people's passions and purpose, through the right economic system, 92
Divine nature, and the Good, True, Beautiful and Right, 87

Economic system and solution, in service of God and Humanity, 89, 91–97
Entropy, corruption and, 89n
Environment and ecosystems, end of destruction and decimation of, through right economic system, 93, 95–96
Equality, America and Islam, and the principle that upholds Humanity, and the world, 85–86
Evil corporations, extensions of evil economic system *see* Monolithic-Monopoly Business
Evolution of Humanity, making political parties obsolete, 90
Evolution of Humanity, the system and, 87

Farms and small businesses, success of, 93, 100
Federal Reserve, *see* Monolithic-Monopoly Business
Freedom of man, John F. Kennedy, coming together for, 83

Gandhi, outer change, just as important to inner change, 87
Gentle Path, 100–101
Globalization, throwing off debt-slave labor and, 91
God, beginning again with, 90
God, concepts aligned with, 86 (*see also* Chapter 1)

God, Humanity's ally against oppressive government, 86
God vs tyranny, 86–87
God's free Earth, and the Gentle Path, 99–101
Good system, following wisdom of, Gandhi and Xiaoping, 87–89
Governing ourselves, another way, and the good system, 100–101
Governing ourselves, another way, through another choice, 100
Government, change of form, for Humanity's happiness, Thomas Jefferson, 84
Government, the choice to amend, dismember, or overthrow, Abraham Lincoln, 84
Government, separation from, 86
Government, weariness of, 87

Happiness, sound economic foundation, and promotion of, 90–96, 100
Happiness, The Spiritual UN and Humanity's, 84
Hemp, natural solution, to replace chemicals and polluting industries, and to detoxify Planet, 100n
Higher Love, and the more perfect union, of Humanity, 90
Holistic world paradigm, zakāt vs income taxes, 96
Holistic World Planetary Paradigm, and the good system, 88–89
Holistic World Planetary Paradigm, necessity of laying down, 88–89
Holistic World Planetary Paradigm, and the separation from War and Militarization, 98–99
Hopi prophecy, and destructive technology, 100n
Human Race, liberation through the American pre-Revolutionary War experience, 101

Humanity's Leading and Self Guiding Principles, 90 (*see also* Chapter 8)
Humanity's time for choice, more of the same, or peace and plenty for all, 88

Income taxes, end of, and the proper basis for taking The People's money, 91–92, 96
Income taxes, the means for total corruption, and destruction, 89, 89n
Indigenous peoples, ending harm to, through right economic system, 93

John F. Kennedy, freedom of man, and coming together, 83
Justice, and the Human family, 86

Love and evolution, inclusion of the poor in, 94

Mammon, division and demise of all, 89, 89n
Mammon and God, two different worlds, 86–88
Mammon, and Humanity's tangible causes for separation from, 97–98
Mammon, push back of, 88
Mammon, the tyranny of, 83–84
Man vs Mammon, 90
Manners and morals, nurturing of, for the better part of ourselves, 95
Manufacturing and trade, sovereign, and the end of slave labor, 95–96
Martin Luther King, Jr, justice, is an intimate universal concern, 86
Money, purpose of, as Creative Oil, 91–92

The Spiritual UN Conceptual Index

Money, serving Man and the well being of the Planet, 90
Monolithic-Monopoly Business, cripples life force of millions of Human beings, 98, 99–100
Monolithic-Monopoly Business, endangers and sickens all, 99
Monolithic-Monopoly Business, extension of usurious economic system, 94n, 97n, 97– 100, 99n, 100n
Monolithic-Monopoly Business, hydra head, petro-chemical-pharma-agri-mining-weapons-war, 99–100
Monolithic-Monopoly Business, making world for profit and war, 98
Monolithic-Monopoly Business, and the monopolization of the Earth, 97–98, 99
Monolithic-Monopoly Business, monopolizing all Human and Earth life, 98–99, 99n
Monolithic-Monopoly Business vs Planetary Consciousness, and the Declaration of Independence, 98
Monolithic-Monopoly Business, replacing of, 99–100
Monolithic-Monopoly Business, separation from, 98–99
Monolithic-Monopoly Business, tyranny of, 100n
Monolithic-Monopoly Business, unhealthy womb, for Planet and Humans, 98, 99
More perfect union, of Humanity, the work of America and Islam, 85
More perfect union, making even more, 90
More perfect union, and putting Mammon in its proper sphere, 88–89

Nations, as sovereign, 95–96

Outer world system, the necessary element for change, 87–88

Peace, holding down of corruption, 87
Perfection vs corruption, 87–88
Perpetual war and terror, Humanity living in error, 88
Political parties, beholden to Mammon world, 89–90
Political parties, obsoleteness of, 90
Poor, Christianity and Islam, and uplifting the, 96
Poor, inclusion of, in Humanity's love and evolution, 94
Poverty, the cause of the American Revolution, 96
Poverty, ending of, through the right economic system, 93

Rich, the problem with, Governor Morris and the, 83 (*see also* Chapter 4, pp 27–32)
Robert F. Kennedy, and the gentle world, 99
Royal Raymond Rife, amazing (holistic) technology of, 94, 94n

Separation from Mammon, Humanity's responsibility to itself, and to the Earth, 97–99, 97n, 99n
Serving of God vs Mammon, the system and, 88
Social Credit, aligns with the economic spiritual principle of "Creative Oil," 92–93
Social Credit, frees and uplifts Humanity, 92–95
Social Credit visionary, Richard Eastman, and the Kingdom of God, 95
Sound economic foundation, and the more perfect union, 90
Sound economic foundation, serves all nations, 91–96
Spiritual path, world choice of, 88
System, and the conditioning to our perfection, 87–88
System is key, to good or evil men, Deng Xiaoping, 87, 89
System, questioning of, Mammon or God, 88

The Spiritual UN Conceptual Index

Technology, end to harmful, 94, 94n
Technology, Hopi Prophecy and, 100n
The Spiritual UN, and the Union, 88
Thomas Jefferson, Founding Fatherly advice, 84
Thomas Jefferson, and governing ourselves without a master, 91

Union and happiness, of Humanity, foremost in American Founding, 83–85
Union, of the Human Race, The Spiritual UN choice of the, 88
US Constitution, Governor Morris and the, 83
US Constitution, the more perfect union, and the Union, 85
Usury, sin, and the ruin of nations and the world, 96–97

War, and technological destruction, choice of world, 88
Wars, organized violence, through the usurious system, 97n
Wars, problems, human needs, and the unsound (fraudulent) economic foundation, 89–90
Wen Jiabo, debt repudiation, an open letter to, 91, 91n
Worker, Environmental and Consumer protections, through sovereign manufacturing and trade, 95–96
World, God and Mammon, and The Spiritual UN, 88
World, ideal, tried and true, through the American pre-Revolutionary War, 101

Zakāt vs the income tax, 96–97

Chapter 10
Abraham Lincoln, and the maturing possibility of all nations, 124–125, 124n–125n

America, *e pluribus unum*, The Spiritual UN, imprinting back on Great Seal of, 128
America and Islam, equality, freedom and God, 121
Atman is Brahman, discovery of a universal Truth, 111
Atom bomb, and the great body of ethical thought, destruction vs creation, 119
Australian aboriginals, uranium mining, and destructive end of the world, 129
Autonomy vs heteronomy, and the economy, 124

Balance of Earth and Humans, structures of wholeness for, 120, 120n
Balance, of feminine and masculine structures, and the path of Love, 107–108
Buddha, weapons and poisons, 122
Buddhism vs Militarism, 112
Bureaucracy, moving on from, 126

Care of the soul, the necessity on Earth, Socrates and, 120
Chief Seattle, and the ethic of the web of life, 129
Chief Seattle, letter to US Government, 112–115
Children, Oneness with God's Earth, teaching, 114
Christ, spirit of, vs laws of men, 118 (*see also* Jesus)
Claude Levi-Strauss, 129
Commons of Man, care and protection of, 128
Conscience, vs dogma and divides, 110, 111
Conscience, the great purpose of, 117
Conscience, and the return to the Oneness of Life, 107
Conscientious objectors, war and, 117
Consciousness, levels of awareness, God, and the Planet, 111

Cosmic consciousness, and the God forward of Evolution, 125–126
Creation, feeling our connectedness with, 117–118
Crossroads, Humanity's common passion vs violence, 126–127

De-militarization of the world, survival, and our choice to the, 128–129
Dharma, of Human being, help not harm, 122 (*also* soul purpose, *also* Human purpose *also* right purpose, *also* essence)
Divinity, seeing all life has, 112

Earth, awareness of, as a Mother, 114, 115–116, 121
Earth, balance, and the great body of ethical thought, 119–120
Earth, evolution and the spiritualizing of, 123–124, 123n (*also* God forward of Evolution)
Earth, and God, all races, respect of, 114, 115
Earth, holistic, aware, self-regulating system, 116
Earth, Humans, and the sacred knowledge, 108n, 109, 111, 111n, 113, 114 (*also* the Sacred Circle)
Earth and Man, dominion, as right relationship, not domination, 114
Earth, relationship, for our wonder and unity, as all Life is linked together, 119
Earth, sacredness of, and the Order of the Universe, 129
Earth, thinking and creativity with the, 119
Earth's natural resources, the necessity to let be, 128–129
Earth's resources, vs the sustenance within, 120–121
Economy, and heteronomy, why we must change the, 124

Ed McGaa, Eagle Man, 122
Ego, third dimensional Earth, and separation from God, 104
Enemies, non-existence of, 124
Energy, laws of physics, free and non-harmful to ecosystems and Earth, 121–122, 122n
Essence, vs ego, and the God-forward of evolution, 119
Essence, of Human being, help not harm, 122 (*also* dharma)
Eternal life, consciousness of, 125
Eternal Spring, path of Love, and the, 108, 108n
Evolution, Darwin vs Teilhard de Chardin, 103
Evolution vs devolution, 104
Evolution, and the great body of ethical thought, 105
Evolution, and Oneness of All Life, Humanity's principles of, 127–128

Family of Universal Man, the great body of ethical thought, and the greater Reality within, 120
Fear, animalistic world, of war and militarism, not true world of Humans, 107
Fearing, "the other," and separation from God, 104
Feminine and masculine structures, balance, and The Spiritual UN, 107–108

Gentle world, knowledge and Human enlightenment, 108n, 111, 111n, 117
George Washington, the cosmic basis of conscience, 107
God, becoming One with, 118 (*also* God consciousness, *see also* Unity consciousness)
God, being within, 123 (*also* Divine Mind also *manas*, *see* Chapter 8, footnote no. 48)

The Spiritual UN Conceptual Index

God, connecting to, 104
God, and conscience, 107
God forward of evolution, equality, social and economic upliftment, and the Natural Earth, 121
God forward of evolution, meeting of Man with God, on Earth, 119 (*see also* Unity consciousness)
God forward of evolution, and the movement of Humanity to cosmic existence, 125
God forward of evolution, pro-human vs Mammon (materiality, greed and selfish desires), 119
God forward of evolution, and the return to the evolutionary track, 126
God forward of evolution, our spiritual selves, and the existence of no harm, 122–123
God, Human and Natural world diversity, in the One, 111
God and the Human's "being," 117
God, Love, and loving, 111–112
God, Religion, and the coming together of Humanity, 111–112
God way, vs greed, corporatism, war, militarism and materialism, 122
Great body of ethical thought, the, 105
Great body of ethical thought, and the divinity of Humanity's unity, 124–125, 124n–125n
Great body of ethical thought, for the enhancement of freedom, 121
Great body of ethical thought, purpose of, 119, 120
Great Human Common Unity, and the planetary initiative, uplift of all, 128
Great Work, of Humanity's diversity, 110

Heart and soul, basis of Humanity's unity, 110
Heaven on Earth, physical meets the metaphysical, 130, 130n
Hermes Trismegistus, 130, 130n
Higher levels of consciousness, and the Planet, discovering our, 106
Higher world, existing in all Human hearts, 105
Holistic World Planetary Paradigm, and The Spiritual UN, of, by and for the people, 104n
Hope, the necessity to remove from the system of War and Militarism, 126–127
Human effort, to War, or to Health of Humanity and Earth, 128–129
Human purpose on Earth, evolution and, 116
Human purpose on Earth, imparting Oneness and Wholeness, through individual uniqueness, 118
Human Race, heart connection, our new experience, 126
Human spirituality, the Planet, and our ultimate unity, in the body of Christ, 109 (Divine life)
Human Union, in the Brotherhood of All, greatest of all, 128
Humanistic world vs animalistic, 103–106
Humanity, new species, moral consciousness and, 125
Humanity, and the Oneness with the Earth, 113, 114
Humanity, and the purpose of diversity, 108–109
Humanity's higher nature, and the body of the Christ, 109
Humanity's other choice, moving off the wrong road, 129–130
Humans, conscience and Earth, 117–118
Humans, and Unity consciousness, 111

Imbalance of Earth, war and, 122
Immanuel Kant, heteronomy vs autonomy, 124
Inner and outer worlds, relationship of, 121,
Inner and outer worlds, spirituality and the, 106
Insights, intuitions and inspirations, the way we are to think, 116 (*see also* Albert Einstein in Chapter 5, p. 43)
Islam, diversity, and the work of the sacred unity, 109–110 (*see also* Nations)
Islam, and the sufficiency of conscience, 110

Jeane Manning, and new energy inventions, 122n
Jesus, belief, teachings, One with God, and moving beyond fear-based, third dimensional existence, 106–107, 107n, 118, 130, 130n
Jihads, greater and lesser, 121 (*see also* jihad in Chapter 3, p. 20)

Knowledge, Human enlightenment, and the gentleness of the world, 108n, 111, 111n, 117

Leader, no need for, 122 (*see also* self-autonomy)
Light, going towards, 104
Love, completeness of, on Earth, 130
Love vs Fear, 103, 106–107, 130
Love, and our inner and outer worlds, relationship, 106
Love, Religion, and the coming together of Humanity, 111–112
Love, and the sacred Oneness of all Life, 106

Mammon, and the destruction of all, 122
Maya, and the world of materiality, 104

Metaphysical order of Earth, Universe, and Reality, 129, 130, 130n
Miracles, and Christ, 106–107, 107n (*see also* Jesus)
Monolithic-Monopoly Business, and the destruction of all, 129, 129n (*see also* Chapter 9)
Monolithic-Monopoly Business, vs Planetary Consciousness, 130
Moral consciousness, and the cosmos, 125
Moral consciousness, remedying world through, 110
Moral realities, 121

National paradigm, the necessity of re-arranging our, 128–129
Nations, great body of ethical thought, and maturing possibility for all, 124–125, 124n–125n
Natural Earth and the God forward of evolution, 121
Nature, reflection of Humanity's virtue, 107–108, 108n

Omega Point, magnet of God, 118
One God, of All, 106
Oneness of All Life, and evolution, Humanity's principles of, 127–128
Oneness of All Life, proper foundation of world, 105
Oneness, consciousness, and Human purpose, 106

Pierre Teilhard de Chardin, 103, 109, 116, 118, 119, 123, 126, 126–127
Placebo effect, health and consciousness, 106
Planet, natural track, swords to ploughshares, 125–126
Planet, and the tectonic shift of unity, 126
Planet, and The Commons of Man, 128 (*see also* Earth and Man)

The Spiritual UN Conceptual Index

Planetary Consciousness, and the caring of the Whole, 130
Planetary Consciousness vs the wrong road, 129–130
Prophets, and the body of ethical thought, purpose of, 117

Questions, the need to ask, to remove cob webs, and, for breakthroughs to truth and evolution of self and world, 116

Religion, God, conscience and Creation, 117–118
Religion, meaning and true purpose of, 104
Religion and morality, purpose of, 105
Religion and science, and the Oneness of All Life, commonality of, 105–106
Religion and science, spirituality bridge between, 106
Religions, all needed, 105
Rich and poor, closing gap between, 121

Sacred order, of Earth and Universe, 129
St Paul, and God, 117
Self-autonomy, equality and, 124 (*also* full autonomous existence)
Seven deadly sins, warning of, 120, 120n
Socrates, 116, 120
Spiritual selves, vs cogs in a machine, 122–123
Spiritual species, the Eternal Spring, and hitting our mark as, 108
Spirituality, bridge between religion and science, 106
Spirituality vs materiality, 122–123, 123n
Standing armies, not our true world, 107 (*see also* War)
Structure, right for Planet, engaging straight from the heart, 126
Structures, to enhance Earth life, 120, 120n

Ten Commandments, vs War, 112
The Spiritual UN, and the attunement to conscience, 107
The Spiritual UN, and the balance of the feminine and masculine aspects of Reality, 107–108
The Spiritual UN, bridge to regain Balance on Planet, 105
The Spiritual UN, higher world, path of heart and, 105
The Spiritual UN, imprinting back on Great Double Sided Seal of America, 128
The Spiritual UN, of, by and for the people, 104n
The Spiritual UN, and the pro-Human way on Earth, 130
The Spiritual UN, and Religion, 104
The Spiritual UN, vs the United Nations, 103–104
Tom Beardon, energy from the vacuum, 122n
Truth, ultimate, questions and, 116
Two Great Commandments, basis for all peace, 112, 112n

Union, Human, greatest of all, 128
Union, perfect and perfecting our, 128
Union, The, perfected, 130
Unity consciousness, ascension to, 111, 117, 118 (*also* God consciousness)
Unity consciousness, and the great Divine Mind, 123 (*see also* Omega Point)
Unity in Diversity, and the One Love, 128
Unity vs homogeneity, 109
Unity, and the individual, ultimate, 109

Vedas, and God, 111, 117

War, the irrational construct of, 122
War, militarism and corporatism, destroying Humans and Planet, 129, 129n

The Spiritual UN Conceptual Index

Wars, destruction, and error existence of Humanity, 114, 123
Wisdom vs sin, 120
World changing paradigm, loving our neighbor as ourselves, 124, 130
World, evolution and happiness of, 104–105
World, Fear and animalistic vs Love and humanistic, 103–106
World, fear and militarism, not true, 107
World peace, Two Great Commandments, basis of, 112, 112n
World, true and the path of The Spiritual UN, 104–105

The Spiritual UN Gentle Path Thesis—"Our Best World" Three Elements

God is light, and in him is no darkness at all.
— 1 John 1:5

Element 1: *Best of* Human life—all is founded, grounded and rooted in the Transcendent value, quality and Reality (God). All works of wisdom, religion and Human liberation are in agreement.

Element 2: Money is the translating medium of the Human essence (metaphysical) to the physical. Its true and proper role is the facilitation of the *best of* Human life—through Human creativity, and creating the *best of* structures, including enlightened education ("Know Thyself"), for the development, encouragement and promotion of Human values, morality and character which have deeper Realities. Money is also the Human effort given to fulfilling the fundamental Human Needs of everyone, everywhere, and no longer to the War "effort"—which is able to confidently exist through the unexamined thought, i.e., **artificial** (concocted) notion and divisions of ethnicities and religions into their "nationalities" with their subsequent states and statelets and egoistic "heads of" states who must now all require, (in the racket of war) weapons over the needs of the people including the children and their futures. In pulling back the cataracts that had been placed over our vision, we find *simply and fundamentally,* we are all <u>one</u> Humanity, all equally carrying the same Divine spark within, and *all* with the *same* needs and wants.

<u>Element 3</u>: Moral framework, the moral consciousness and the moral way (the indivisible Good, True Beautiful and Right that brooks no contradictions) are our Best World through the real world of real freedom. It promotes, encourages, allows the *best of* Human life with the effects of happiness, liberty, peace, palpable freedom, abundance, creativity, innovation and inventions in our now flourishing world (that no longer has any "political" prisoners, has little government, no more bureaucracies, and no more harm to the Planet).

Our Best World is seen to be the free flow of the metaphysical to the physical—and from the inner to the outer. Within the free flow is the Source of our happiness, liberty, peace, freedom, abundance, creativity, innovation, invention and now, planet-wide, inner and outer fulfillment. Without the free flow, we don't have the world we have been designed for (through our dharma, i.e., our essence, our Human purpose or our right function as

Humans) and therefore, we will never be, can be at peace (both inner and outer) until these <u>three elements</u> are laid down as it naturally includes economic and social justice.

Matured times now call for the matured Human Race, to Begin Again, now, from our best place—our Best World Three Elements as the new conscious starting point—or be condemned to the same sorry and hellish world, doing over and over again, with War and violence, and expecting a different result, which Einstein said, was the definition of insanity.

Our effort must be collective, as simply the one Human Family, and doing for others that what we wish for ourselves from the point of our Equality, as Martin Luther King Jr rightly said:

> *"Injustice anywhere is a threat to justice everywhere. We are caught in an inescapable network of mutuality, tied in a single garment of destiny. Whatever affects one directly, affects all indirectly."*

And thus, what he said in his time, as the challenge facing the modern man, still holds true for the Human Race at this time on this Planet:

> *"I believe today that there is a need for all people of good will to come together with a massive act of conscience and say in the words of the old Negro spiritual, "We ain't goin' study war no more"*
> —in Justice for all.

Reflections

Reflections

www.ingramcontent.com/pod-product-compliance
Lightning Source LLC
Chambersburg PA
CBHW070947180426
43194CB00041B/1658